Basic Quiltmaking Techniques

for Curved Piecing

Paulette Peters

Martingale
& COMPANY

Bothell, Washington

Credits

President . . . . Nancy J. Martin
CEO/Publisher . . . . Daniel J. Martin
Associate Publisher . . . . Jane Hamada
Editorial Director . . . . Mary V. Green
Design and
    Production Manager . . . . . Cheryl Stevenson
Technical Editor . . . . Christine Barnes
Copy Editor . . . . Tina Cook
Illustrator . . . . Laurel Strand
Photographer . . . . Brent Kane
Cover Designer . . . . Magrit Baurecht
Text Designer . . . . Kay Green
Proofreader . . . . Leslie Phillips

Dedication

To quiltmakers who are ready to take another step in refining their skills. May curved piecing add to your versatility and your ability to create any design you wish.

Acknowledgments

Thanks to Carol Doak, for *Your First Quilt Book (or it should be!)* and for responding to the needs of new quilters. Thanks to Ursula Reikes at Martingale & Company for her professional expertise, to Christine Barnes for bringing order from chaos, and to Laurel Strand for her skill at drawing curves on the computer.

Basic Quiltmaking Techniques
for Curved Piecing
© 1999 by Paulette Peters

Martingale & Company
PO Box 118
Bothell, WA 98041-0118 USA

Printed in the United States of America
03 02 01 00 99 98   6 5 4 3 2 1

MISSION STATEMENT

WE ARE DEDICATED TO PROVIDING QUALITY PRODUCTS AND SERVICE BY WORKING TOGETHER TO INSPIRE CREATIVITY AND TO ENRICH THE LIVES WE TOUCH.

Library of Congress Cataloging-in-Publication Data
Peters, Paulette
    Basic quiltmaking techniques for curved piecing / Paulette Peters.
        p. cm.
    Includes bibliographical references (p.).
    ISBN 1-56477-252-7
    1. Patchwork—Patterns. 2. Quilting—Patterns.
3. Seams (Sewing) I. Title.
TT835.P449126 1999
746.46—dc21   98-42875
                                                      CIP

Contents

Foreword

Guess what? All your patchwork seams do not need to be straight! They can be curved, and a curved seam does not need to be feared, even by beginning quiltmakers. As you'll discover on the following pages, curved piecing is just another creative avenue for making patchwork projects.

Basic Quiltmaking Techniques for Curved Piecing builds on what you learned in *Your First Quilt Book (or it should be!)* and expands your design options. Quilt patterns that look difficult can be pieced, without frustration, using either hand or machine methods.

Paulette begins with the basics of marking, cutting, and sewing curved shapes. If you have Paulette's other book in the series, *Basic Quiltmaking Techniques for Strip Piecing,* you are already familiar with her easygoing, conversational style. Her simple, step-by-step instructions for the curved-piecing process show you just how easy it is to create curved patchwork.

Paulette has created eight wonderful patchwork projects geared for beginning curved piecing, whether stitched by hand or machine. You might like to start with the pillow, then work your way to the more challenging projects. All are fast and fun.

If you're new to curved piecing, now is a great time to add to your quiltmaking skills. If you're a more experienced quiltmaker, I know you will enjoy stitching one or more of Paulette's projects. You'll also find instructions for drawing curved piecing patterns, when you're ready to design your own. Whatever your level of expertise, I am confident you will enjoy this new patchwork avenue. Have fun with curves!

Carol Doak

Introduction

I wrote *Basic Quiltmaking Techniques for Curved Piecing* to complement *Your First Quilt Book (or it should be!)* by Carol Doak. If you worked through Carol's book, you have developed basic quiltmaking skills. The book you now hold in your hands builds on those skills and explores the special technique of curved piecing. It's designed as a reference, available whenever you are ready to go "around the bend."

Many beginning quilters come to quiltmaking classes with the desire to make a Double Wedding Ring quilt. They are soon discouraged because they are told that curves are too difficult for new quiltmakers. I won't deceive you: curved piecing is an acquired skill. It takes a little time to learn this technique, but there are ways to make it easier, and it's definitely worth doing.

When I browse through my books on antique quilts, I'm always attracted to the quilts with curves. They look so complex, with lines that flow from one area to another, leading the eye across the surface. Curved designs are prettier, gentler, and softer than straight-line piecing. In contemporary designs, they can knock your socks off! Learning to "do curves" will add to your quiltmaking versatility. Trust me: if you can piece curves, you can piece anything.

I've chosen classic block designs for easy practice. I'll guide you through the steps that work best for me, and give you several approaches to the curved-piecing technique. I hope you'll take the time to decide which methods work best for you and to make some of these beautiful quilt blocks. As you are about to learn, there's no need to avoid a quilt pattern you love because it has curves and looks difficult. You can do this!

Paulette Peters

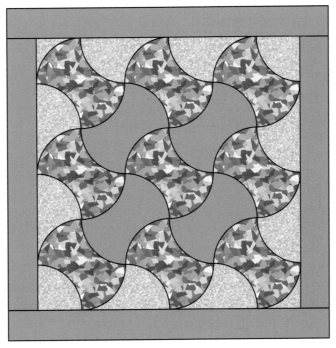

How to Use This Book

I suggest you begin by reading "Curved-Piecing Principles" (page 11) and "Curved-Piecing Techniques" (page 13). In these chapters, you'll find an overview of the techniques for curved piecing, a few goals to aim for, and several approaches to stitching your first curve. Gather the tools you'll need and a few of your favorite fabrics, pick a project, and start "piecing a-round."

As you gain experience, I know you'll want to adapt these blocks to different sizes. When you're ready to design your own quilt, refer to the suggestions in "Designing Patterns with Curves" (page 21).

You will find three symbols as you read:

Tip boxes offer helpful hints to make the process easier. Read these right away.

Alert boxes let you know when you need to be careful. Your guardian angel will help you avoid potential snags.

Down the Road (DTR) boxes provide information for future quiltmaking projects, after you have more experience. Refer to these special features when you're ready to explore a bit more.

Glossary:
The Language of Curved Piecing

Bias grain: The grain line that runs at a 45° angle to the selvage. The bias is the stretchiest part of the fabric.

Block: A unit created by sewing patches together. This is the basic design unit in most quilts.

Blocking: Sizing a finished block by pressing it to shape or by trimming it (only if *really* necessary). Also known as squaring-up.

Chain piecing: Sewing patches consecutively without cutting the threads between them. Also known as fast feeding.

Curved piecing: Sewing patchwork pieces along a curved seam line, by hand or by machine.

Fat quarters: Pre-cut fabric pieces approximately 18" x 22", rather than 9" across the width of the bolt. Most quilt shops sell fat quarters. This cut gives quilters more usable fabric for cutting block pieces.

Registration marks: Marks on a template or a piece of fabric that indicate where to match a seam before sewing.

Rotary cutter: A tool for cutting straight lines (easy for everyone) and curves (if you're really good). In curved piecing, you will use your rotary cutter to cut the straight edges of block pieces.

Seam allowance: Extra fabric beyond the sewing line that allows you to join patchwork pieces. The standard seam allowance for patchwork is ¼" on all sides of each shape.

Selvage: The tightly woven lengthwise edge of the fabric. Cut the selvage off before cutting your block pieces.

Straight grain: The grain line that runs parallel to the selvage (lengthwise grain), or from selvage to selvage (crosswise grain).

Template: A pattern piece made from stiff material such as plastic. You place a template on your fabric and trace around it.

Unit: A section of a quilt block that is repeated and joined to other units or pieces.

Tools and Supplies

You'll find a complete list of quilting tools in *Your First Quilt Book*. The following tools make curved piecing easier:

Compass: When you're ready to design your own curved pieces, invest in a good-quality compass. (See "Designing Patterns with Curves" on page 21.)

Clear plastic rulers: A ruler marked with a ⅛" grid is indispensable. The 2" x 18" ruler is most useful, but the 12" ruler is great for taking to workshops. Use your ruler to add seam allowances to curves and to design patterns, but never use it to cut with your rotary cutter.

Flexible curve: You'll find this tool in art supply stores. (See "Designing Patterns with Curves" on page 21.)

Flexible tape: Use ¼"-wide yellow masking tape to mark a curve for hand quilting. This tape is available in quilt stores and through mail-order catalogs.

Iron and accessories: A dry iron, set on cotton, works best for me because steam irons, especially those with automatic shut-offs, spit on my fabric at just the wrong moment. I keep a spray bottle of water next to the ironing board for misting seams. Press the seams dry if necessary.

If a fabric is soft and stretchy, I use spray sizing from the grocery store. Spray sizing firms up fabric but isn't as heavy as spray starch.

Marking pens and pencils: Use a permanent, ultra-fine pen for writing on templates and for marking the cutting line when you use cut-size templates for machine piecing. Check to make sure the ink doesn't show through on the right side of the fabric. The pen should make a very fine line, with no bleeding. Use a pen with permanent ink so your marks won't run in the wash after the quilt is finished. A

mechanical pencil with soft lead that doesn't drag as it moves along the template edge is useful for marking around templates on light fabric. Use a pencil with hard lead for drafting patterns. A white, silver, or yellow chalk pencil or colored pencil that can hold a sharp point is useful for marking around templates on dark fabric. Every fabric reacts differently to marking pens and pencils. Test your marker before marking any of your pieces!

Do not use a ballpoint pen to mark fabric, even on the wrong side. If you wash the project, the ink may run and ruin the piece.

Patchwork foot: If your machine has a ¼" presser foot, use it. If not, add the foot to your "wish list." It's a wonderful attachment for feeding curves smoothly into the machine.

Take care of your machine; it's your best friend. Each time you start a new project, clean and oil your machine, put in a new needle, and give your machine a kiss. Clean out the lint every time you change the bobbin. Both of you will be happier and perform better. Most machine dealers offer regular maintenance checkups, which can do great things for your tension.

Pins: Use long, thin straight pins, either fine silk or glass-head pins, for joining seams. Heavy pins with plastic heads displace fabric.

Needles: For hand piecing, use a size 10 quilting needle. A short needle equals short stitches; a long needle equals long stitches and ruffles in the curved seam. For machine piecing woven fabric, use a size 80/12 needle.

Thread: For hand and machine piecing, medium-weight sewing thread, preferably all-cotton, is strong and durable and lies snugly in the seam. Quilting thread is too heavy for piecing. When piecing by hand, cut the thread in lengths no longer than 15" to 18". Longer lengths tangle easily, and the thread wears out as you pull it through the fabric. It's also a hazard to the person sitting next to you at a meeting. For both hand and machine piecing, choose a neutral-color thread that blends with both fabrics. If one fabric is very light and the other is very dark, use a dark thread.

Rotary cutter: Use the medium-size (45mm) rotary cutter for straight-line cutting through several layers. Keep extra blades on hand so you can replace a blade as soon as it gets dull. For the projects in this book, you won't rotary cut curves. If you want to try rotary cutting curves once you're more experienced, use the smaller (35mm) cutter.

Cutting mat: Use a mat with a grid for measuring. Buy the largest size you can use on your cutting surface, at least 18" x 24".

Treat your rotary cutter and mat with respect. Close the rotary cutter every time you set it down—you don't have time for first aid. Of course, always keep it away from children. Rotary mats are prone to curling permanently in heat. Store your mat flat, if possible, and never leave it in a hot car.

Rotary rulers: Use these acrylic rulers for cutting borders and straight edges of patches. Here's a list of necessary rulers:

• A 24"-long ruler marked in ¼" increments. Use this ruler to cut strips across the width of the fabric. I prefer the one without the lip that hooks over the mat.
• An 8" square ruler with a right-angle mark. My favorite is the Bias Square® ruler from Martingale & Company. This ruler is convenient for cutting smaller pieces from strips before using a template to cut the curves.

Scissors: A good-quality, sharp pair of scissors is a must for curved piecing. Use your good scissors on fabric only; get a cheaper pair and designate them for paper cutting or template cutting. Then threaten jail time for any family member who uses your fabric-cutting scissors for paper.

Seam ripper (or un-sewer): Use your seam ripper as an extra finger to hold curved seams in place as you feed them into the machine. Choose a seam ripper with a fine point and replace it regularly. They get dull, just like scissors.

To quickly remove a seam, work on the bobbin side of the seam. Snip every third or fourth stitch along the length of the seam. Turn the piece over and pull the top thread. This method is quick, but messy; you'll need to brush off the thread wisps.

Template plastic: A good, sturdy plastic template will see you through many quilt pieces. Semi-transparent, flexible plastic, either plain or gridded, is the best material for templates. It is available in most fabric and quilt shops. I prefer to use clear plastic because I can see through it and it's somewhat flexible. White plastic is also good, although it's more difficult to cut. Don't use cardboard unless you're planning to cut just a few pieces. Cardboard, poster board, and sandpaper edges soften, and the shape is soon distorted.

⅛" hole punch: Available in office supply stores, this punch has a finer tip than the usual paper punch.

¼" marking devices: It's tricky to add an accurate seam allowance to an irregular curve. Try a ¼" clear plastic straight tool or a clear ruler with ¼" markings that can be moved along the edge of the curve in small increments. You can also use a ¼" metal rolling circle that moves along the edge of a template, guided by a pencil point.

Fabric Selection

Selecting fabrics is one of the most exciting and challenging aspects of quiltmaking. Following are a few guidelines for choosing fabric when you're ready to "go curvy."

Fiber Content

Curved piecing behaves best with 100% cotton fabric. Cotton stretches slightly when you need it to, and it presses into crisp seams. If you need to clip a seam allowance, cotton is less likely to fray or ravel than other fabrics. Avoid using fabrics that contain polyester. Polyester threads do not bend softly, seam allowances don't lie smoothly around curves, and edges fray.

Color

As you choose fabrics for curved piecing, consider the following aspects of color and design. Take your time when you select fabrics and be willing to try new and unusual combinations. A little extra time spent at the planning stage always pays off.

Contrast

Color, or hue, isn't as important to quilters as "How dark is it?" or "How light is it?" I use higher-contrast fabrics in curved piecing than in straight piecing because a curved line visually blends fabrics more than a straight line. High contrast between fabrics on each side of a curve makes the curve more visible, while low contrast blurs the curve. Test the contrast by auditioning fabrics side by side.

Visual Texture

Curved piecing presents wonderful opportunities for visual texture. Textured fabrics add an organic, or natural, element to a quilt. Look for fabrics that contribute to that effect, such as prints with swirly lines, small- or large-scale floral prints, or atmospheric prints that look like sky, clouds, water, or earth. Keep the following points in mind as you choose textured fabrics:

• A large-scale, swirly floral print can create a dappled, watercolor look in places where the curved design lines in the fabric intersect curves in the block. (See "True Lover's Knot" on page 25.)

• An active, lively print with curved design lines accentuates curved piecing and suggests movement. (See "Double Ax" on page 28.)

• Geometric prints such as plaids and stripes are wonderful in curved piecing. Decide which direction the straight lines will go before you cut the pieces. Use the grain-line arrows to position the template on the fabric.

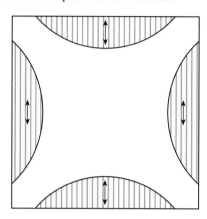

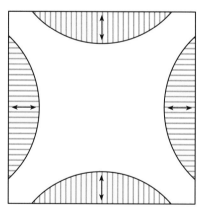

Curved-Piecing Principles

Let's start with the principles of curved piecing. Understanding how curves behave will make stitching them easier and a lot more fun.

Concave and Convex Curves

Every curve has an "innie" side, called concave (it caves in), and an "outie" side, called convex (it curves out).

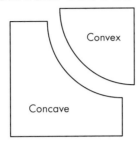

The seam allowances on each side behave differently. On the concave side of the curve, the seam allowance is tight, with little "give." When you press the seam allowances toward the concave piece, you will need to clip the underneath seam allowance. On the convex side of the curve, the seam allowance is poufy, with lots of extra fabric. When you press the seam allowances toward the convex piece, the underneath seam allowance will be poufy.

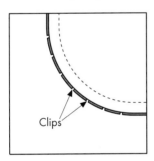

Seam allowance pressed toward concave piece

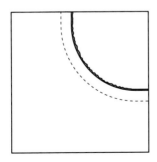

Seam allowance pressed toward convex piece

Wide Curves and Tight Curves

The "degree of curve" has to do with how wide or tight a curve is. The more open or gentle the curve, the easier it is to piece. An arc based on a true circle can be pieced accurately, but the degree of difficulty increases as the size of the circle decreases. A simple Mariner's Compass block is an example of a large circle set into a square background.

Portions of circles are used in the classic Drunkard's Path block.

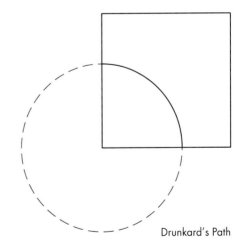

Drunkard's Path

In the same block, using an arc from a larger circle creates a broader, gentler curve. (See "Designing Patterns with Curves" on page 21.)

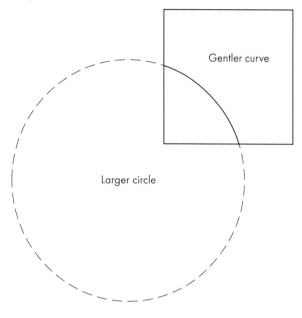

The projects in this book will give you the opportunity to try curves of different degrees.

Grain Line

Grain line is very important in curved piecing. The goal is to keep the grain lines running in the same direction they would run if the block were all one piece of fabric. This orientation takes the curve across both the bias and the straight grain, so some areas are stretchy and some are stable.

The templates in this book are marked with an arrow indicating the straight of grain, either lengthwise or crosswise.

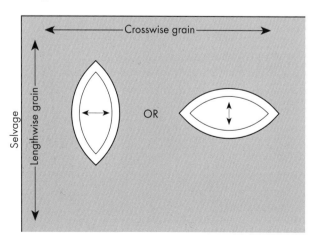

Sew a Fine (Curved) Seam

Before you begin to piece curved shapes, consider these two goals:

• Try to get a smooth, crisp curve, with no wobbles or flat areas.

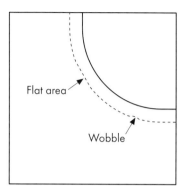

You can accomplish this by exactly matching the seam lines on each piece. When hand piecing, keep checking both the front and the back. When machine piecing, sew slowly and maintain an exact ¼"-wide seam allowance.

• Strive to achieve even distribution of fabric along the curve, with no puckers or pleats. You can accomplish this with registration marks. Match the ends and the middle of the curve. Longer curved seams may require more registration marks. (See "Curved-Piecing Techniques," following.)

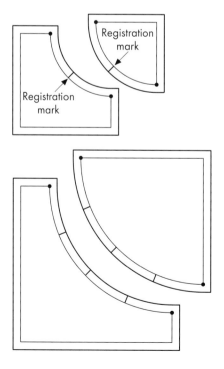

Curved-Piecing Techniques

You can successfully piece curved shapes by hand sewing or machine sewing. At times it is efficient to combine the two techniques: hand sew a tight curve, and then machine piece the block. Using the following hints, you'll soon be doing "wheelies" and S's and you'll never have to avoid a wonderful pattern because it has curves.

Templates

For a rotary-cutting fanatic like me, templates are a step back. But it's essential to mark curves before cutting or piecing them, and templates make quick work of it. See "Tools and Supplies" on page 9 for a discussion of template material.

Accurate templates are essential in curved piecing. Remember that every pencil line adds to the size of the template, and drawing around the template adds another pencil line to the quilt piece. Use your paper-cutting scissors to cut carefully on the drawn line, leaving most of the line on the excess template material.

Template Style

You'll find three kinds of templates used throughout this book: finished-size templates, cut-size templates, and combination templates. For special situations, you may also want to make window templates. Each project tells you the type of template I used, but you can decide which is most appropriate for your working method.

• **Finished-size template (without seam allowances).** This template is used for traditional hand piecing, and registration marks are inside the template edge. Do not cut a notch in the template edge. Instead, draw around the template on the wrong side of the fabric, marking the registration marks just outside the

drawn line. Mark a dot where the curved seam starts and ends. Cut approximately ¼" beyond the drawn line to add the seam allowance.

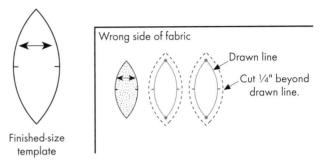

Finished-size template

Wrong side of fabric — Drawn line — Cut ¼" beyond drawn line.

• **Cut-size template (with seam allowances).** Use this template for machine piecing. I trace the seam line on the template to remind me that the seam allowance has already been added. Registration marks are in the seam allowance of the template. Cut a tiny notch at each registration mark. When you draw around the template on the wrong side of the fabric, let the marker drop into the notch.

For many patterns, you also need to know where the seam starts and ends. Punch a hole at the corner of the template where the seam lines intersect, using a ⅛" punch. (See "Tools and Supplies" on page 9.) Place the punch so that most of the hole is in the seam allowance.

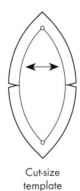
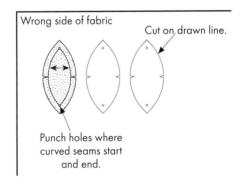

Cut-size template

Wrong side of fabric — Cut on drawn line. Punch holes where curved seams start and end.

• **Combination template.** A combination template has seam allowances on the straight sides and no seam allowances on the curves. Add a dot to the template where the curved seam starts and ends. Don't forget to cut ¼" beyond the curve after you mark it.

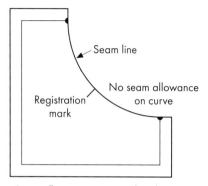

Combination template

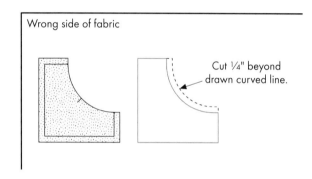

Repeat after me: "I promise not to cut the curves on the drawn lines. I will remember to cut ¼" beyond the curved lines I have drawn."

• **Window template.** A window template is just what it sounds like, a shape with a cut-out "window." When you place a window template over fabric, the window shows what the finished piece will look like. This template has advantages for hand piecing and machine piecing. It allows you to draw a sewing line for hand piecing and cut an accurate ¼" seam allowance. In machine piecing some curves, such as an S-shape, a visual sewing line is helpful. The disadvantage is that the template is somewhat weak and distorts easily as you draw around it. Commercial window templates made from metal are great if the size you need is available.

Cutting a window template is easier if you cut through one spot on the template, cut out the center, then tape the cut closed.

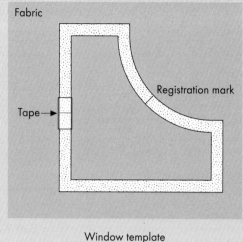

Window template

To review template styles, let's take a look at a finished-size, a cut-size, and a combination template for the same curved piece. Note that the finished-size template has no seam allowances, while the cut-size template does. The combination template has seam allowances on the straight edges, but no seam allowance on the curve.

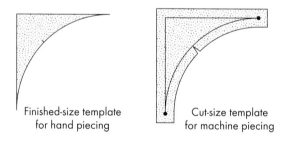

Finished-size template for hand piecing

Cut-size template for machine piecing

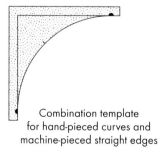

Combination template for hand-pieced curves and machine-pieced straight edges

Let's take another look at the different kinds of templates used in this book. They have inner and outer lines. Here's what those lines mean:

Finished size templates: Cut the template on the inner lines.

Cut-size templates: Cut the template on the outer lines.

Combination templates: Cut the template on the outer lines. Then cut away the seam allowance from the curved edge (inner line).

Window templates: Cut the template on both lines.

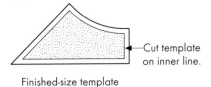

Finished-size template

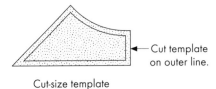

Cut-size template

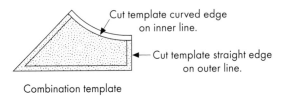

Combination template

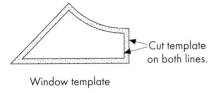

Window template

How to Make a Template

Method 1 uses transparent plastic template material.

1. Use removable tape to fasten the plastic template material to the page, over the shapes.

2. With a fine-tipped permanent marker, trace the pieces on the plastic, marking the registration marks and grain lines. Be sure to use the appropriate lines for the template style you have chosen.

3. Carefully cut on the marked lines. Check the accuracy by placing the template on the pattern.

4. For a finished-size or combination template, mark the registration marks. For a cut-size template, cut notches at the edge at each registration mark and punch holes where the seams intersect.

Method 2 uses material other than transparent plastic.

1. Trace the template on a piece of paper. Don't cut on the template lines yet.

2. Glue the paper to a piece of template plastic with a gluestick.

3. Carefully cut out the template on the cutting lines. Check the accuracy by placing the template on the pattern.

4. Follow step 4, above, to mark registration marks and punch holes where the seams intersect.

Cutting Curved Pieces

Use your good scissors for cutting curves. Heavy plastic or metal templates are available for some curved patterns, and these can be used with a rotary cutter. However, templates made from typical template material will not guide a rotary cutter for a smooth cut. You may choose to draw a curved line on the fabric, then cut the line freehand with a rotary cutter. If so, use the small blade (35mm), which will track a curve better than a larger blade. This technique takes a firm hand and some practice.

Because of the speed and accuracy of rotary cutting, I prefer to combine it with hand cutting. All the straight lines in a pattern can be "rotary-ed," while the curves are scissor-cut.

For speed, many of the projects in this book direct you to rotary cut shapes such as squares or rectangles and to cut curved pieces from those shapes. This technique wastes small amounts of fabric, but the time saved and the ease of controlling the grain line is worth the bit of fabric discarded.

Curved Piecing by Hand

Hand piecing is best for tight curves and small pieces. Hand piecing has several advantages: It's portable, allowing you to take your work wherever you go. Hand piecing has a meditative quality, providing you with joy in the process. You can also control the seam line with hand piecing to an extent not always possible with machine piecing.

See "Tools and Supplies" on pages 8–9 for tips on choosing the appropriate needle and thread. For a complete discussion of hand piecing, refer to *Your First Quilt Book*.

Follow these simple steps to sew curved pieces by hand:

1. On the wrong side of the fabric, draw around a finished-size template for each piece. This line is the seam line—*not the cutting line*. Leave at least ½" between pieces for the seam allowances. Mark registration marks outside the template, where the seam allowances will be. Mark a dot where the curved seam starts and ends. Be sure to heed the grain-line arrow.

2. Cut ¼" beyond the drawn line. This seam allowance may be "guesstimated" or accurately drawn with a window template (page 14) or a ¼" marking device (page 9). The seam allowance width is less important than the seam line, but I like to cut the seam allowance exactly ¼" wide to enable me to line up the edges easily.

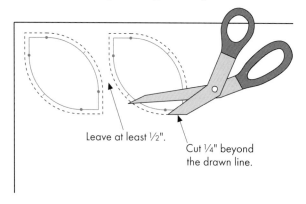

Leave at least ½".

Cut ¼" beyond the drawn line.

3. Pinning curved pieces for hand sewing is an art form. It looks as though the edges will never fit together, but they will. At first, you will feel comfortable using lots of pins. As you gain experience, you can get by with fewer pins. Insert the pin straight into the drawn seam line or dot and straight out the other drawn seam line or dot. While turning the pin down into the work, hold the pieces firmly to keep them from slipping.

   a. Pin the dot at one end of the seam, matching both sides.

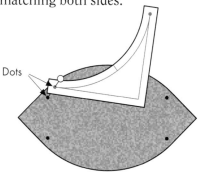

Dots

   b. Pin the registration marks, matching both sides.

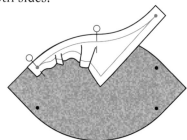

   c. Pin the other end of the seam at the dot. Continue pinning at intervals between each registration mark until the seam settles into place.

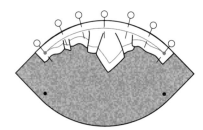

4. Curve the pinned pieces over your finger as you sew. I sew with the concave piece on top and the fullness of the convex piece underneath. Try it both ways to see which you prefer.

5. Begin sewing at the corner dot. Do not sew across the seam allowance. Leaving a tail of the thread unknotted, take 1 small stitch, then another stitch in the same place. While the thread is still looped, slip your needle through the loop, then pull the loop down tightly. The thread won't slip out of this end.

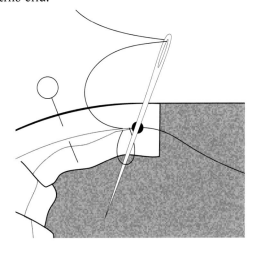

6. Take 2 or 3 stitches on the needle, checking to be sure the back is still aligned with the front. Pull the needle through. Backstitch every 4 or 5 stitches to stabilize the seam. Remove pins as the needle approaches them.

To help keep your thread from twisting and knotting, pull the needle out in the same direction you are stitching. Don't pull the needle up or back.

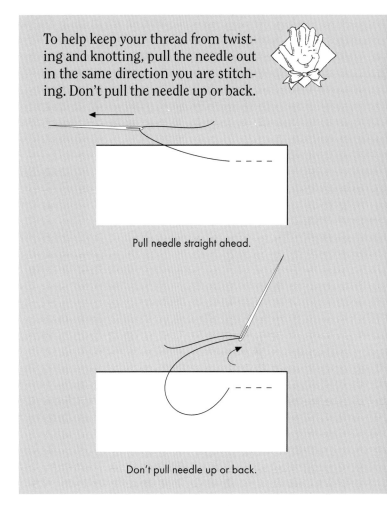

Pull needle straight ahead.

Don't pull needle up or back.

7. Finish the end of the seam at the dot in the same way you started: take a small stitch, then another small stitch, and pull the needle through the loop to fasten the thread off.

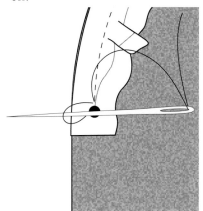

Curved Piecing by Machine

Curved piecing by machine has several advantages: It's speedy, and the seams are strong, making for a sturdy project. Machine piecing is best for shallow, gentle curves and large pieces. See "Tools and Supplies" (pages 8–9) for tips on choosing the appropriate needle and thread.

Machine Settings

To make your stitching easier, set your machine as follows:

Stitch length: The average setting on most machines is fine for curved piecing, but shortening the stitch may help you sew a smoother seam, particularly if the curve is tight.

Needle down: Use this setting if your machine has it. If it doesn't, get in the habit of stopping with the needle down in the fabric each time you pause.

Slow speed: Many machines have a setting that allows you to sew at half speed, even if you have a "heavy driving foot." Use this setting to keep focused and to make your machine more efficient.

Seam guide: Determine where your machine sews an exact ¼"-wide seam allowance and mark it.

Follow these simple steps to sew curved pieces by machine:

1. On the wrong side of the fabric, draw around a cut-size template that has notches for the registration marks. (See "Templates" on page 13.) Heed the grain-line arrow. Let the marker drop into the notch at each registration mark. Mark dots through the holes you punched where the curved seams start and end.

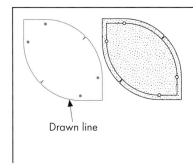

Drawn line

2. Cut smoothly on the drawn line. Do not cut into the notch; the mark is sufficient.
3. The number of pins, if any, depends on the size and angle of the curve. One pin at the center registration mark and at each end is usually sufficient for machine piecing.

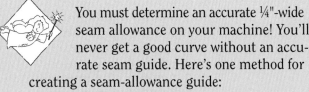

You must determine an accurate ¼"-wide seam allowance on your machine! You'll never get a good curve without an accurate seam guide. Here's one method for creating a seam-allowance guide:

1. Place a rotary ruler under the presser foot.
2. Gently drop the needle onto the ¼" line.
3. Lower the presser foot to hold the ruler in place.
4. Align the edge of the ruler so it is straight, from front to back.

5. Place several layers of masking tape along the edge of the ruler to create a seam guide. Sew a sample seam and measure from the seam line to the cut edge. It should be exactly ¼".

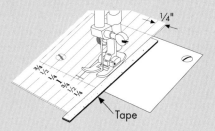

¼"

Tape

4. Place the concave piece on the top, and the convex piece underneath. It looks as though the edges never will fit together, but they will. Place a pin at the dot, matching the dot on the convex piece.

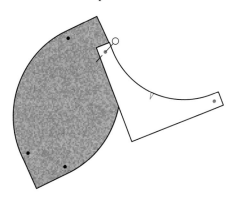

5. Swing the edge of the pieces into alignment with the ¼" seam guide on the machine. Begin sewing at the edge, tapering across the seam allowance. Do not backstitch. Take 2 or 3 stitches and stop with the needle down. Keep your eyes on where you're going, watching the edges of the fabric pieces and the seam guide, not where the needle is going up and down. Slowly sew several more stitches. Place a pin at the center registration mark.

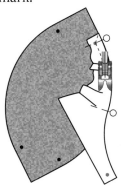

6. Again swing the edges into alignment with the ¼" seam guide. Repeat the process to the end of the seam, tapering across the seam allowance. Chain piece the units if desired.

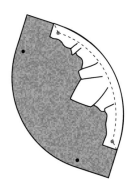

As you sew, use a seam ripper or a pin to nudge the edges into alignment and hold them in place.

Check the smoothness of your curve before pressing it. If there are flat spots or bumps, correct them before ironing them. Many times, misshapen seams are the result of an inaccurate ¼" seam allowance on one side of the curve or the other. It's usually easier to remove the entire seam and start again. The curve will be smoother than patching the seam here and there.

Combined Techniques

If you are using combination templates to hand piece the curves and machine piece the straight edges, follow these simple steps:

1. On the wrong side of the fabric, draw around the combination template for each piece. Leave at least ½" between pieces. (You should have already trimmed the seam allowance from the curved edge of your template.) On the curve, the drawn line is the seam line—*not the cutting line*. On the straight edges, the drawn lines are the cutting lines. Mark the registration marks. Mark a dot where the curved seam starts and ends.

2. Cut ¼" beyond the marked curve to add the seam allowance. Cut on the straight lines.

3. Follow steps 3–7 of "Curved Piecing by Hand" (pages 16–17) to hand piece the curved seam.

4. Machine piece the straight edges.

Pressing Curved Seams

Press curved seams from the front of the piece, to ensure a crisp line with no pleats. Use a dry iron. In general, press the seam allowance toward the convex side of the curve.

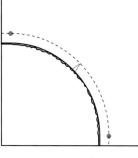

Wrong side

Pressing toward the convex side causes the seam allowance to form little "ruffles" as it folds around the curve. If the curve is gentle and the fabric is soft, these ruffles are no problem. If the curve is tight or the fabric is stiff, use one of the following methods to "unruffle" the seam and reduce the bulk:

Method 1: Press the seam, letting ruffles form where they will. At each ruffle on the convex curve, make a small clip straight into the seam allowance, about ⅛". Press again.

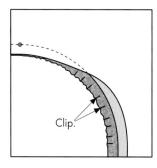

Clip.

Method 2: Trim the edge of the convex seam allowance with pinking shears to form little notches that lie evenly around the curve. Use this method after the seam is sewn because you need that smooth edge for sewing an accurate ¼"-wide seam allowance.

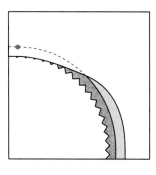

Occasionally, you will want to press the seam allowance toward the concave side of a curve. For example, if you have a lighter fabric on the convex side, or you want to quilt in the ditch on the convex side, you'll want to press the seam allowance toward the concave side.

You may also want to press toward the concave side to turn a seam allowance to interlock with an adjoining one. In these situations, clipping is a must.

Before pressing, carefully make several clips with your scissors tip, at evenly spaced intervals along the curve, through the concave seam allowance only. Clip straight toward the seam line, to within two to three threads of the seam line, and use only as many clips as necessary to allow the seam to lie flat. Press.

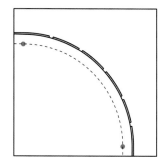

Blocking Your Blocks

A curved seam within a block can distort the block, making it less square than you'd hoped for. Bring it back to shape with a blocking square.

1. Draw a square on a piece of paper, the finished size plus seam allowances. To make a 6" finished block, for example, draw a 6½" square. Use pencil or permanent pen, not ballpoint.

2. Place the paper on the ironing board. Anchor one corner of the block by pinning through the paper into the ironing board cover. Gently pull the other corners into place and anchor each corner with a pin. Using a steam iron, press firmly. Allow the block to cool before releasing the pins. It's called "creative pressing," and it squares blocks so they fit their neighbors.

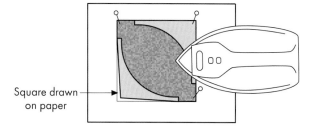

Square drawn on paper

Are you ready to begin a curved-piecing project? Turn to page 33 to choose a design and start sewing curves! Come back to the following section for reference.

Designing Patterns with Curves

When you're ready to change the size of one of the patterns in this book or to design your own curved pattern, put on your designer's hat and work through this section.

Choosing a Compass

A good compass can be tightened with a screw apparatus that will hold the compass securely at your measurement. You can find good-quality compasses at an art supply or office supply store. Don't try to use the inexpensive slide ones kids take to school; they will lead to much frustration. A bar compass is a good tool for large circles or arcs. You can extend it to draw large patterns and tighten it to any measurement. Some rulers have holes every ¼". These will draw a good circle, but they limit the measurements you can use.

Drawing a Curved Pattern

Many curved quilt patterns start with a square, with the curves drawn from points on or outside the square. Begin by drawing a square on ¼" graph paper. For large patterns, tape several sheets of paper together, aligning the graph lines, or use a large desk pad that is printed with graph paper, available at office supply stores. Work on a pad of paper or on your rotary cutting mat to give the compass point something to grab.

Let's begin with a simple exercise. Suppose you want to make a "True Lover's Knot" quilt (page 60), but with 6" blocks.

1. Draw a square, 6" x 6", on the graph paper. Do this in ink.
2. Draw a square, 1" x 1", in 2 opposite corners, also in ink.

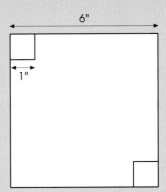

3. Place the point of the compass on a corner that does not have a 1" square. Open the compass until its pencil touches the point of a small square. Tighten the screw. Draw an arc from one small square to the opposite small square. Because you drew the squares in ink, you'll be able to erase the curved pencil line if necessary.

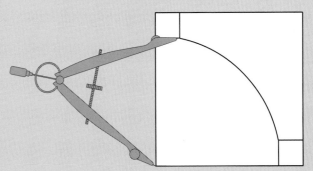

4. Place the point of the compass in the opposite corner and repeat the arc.

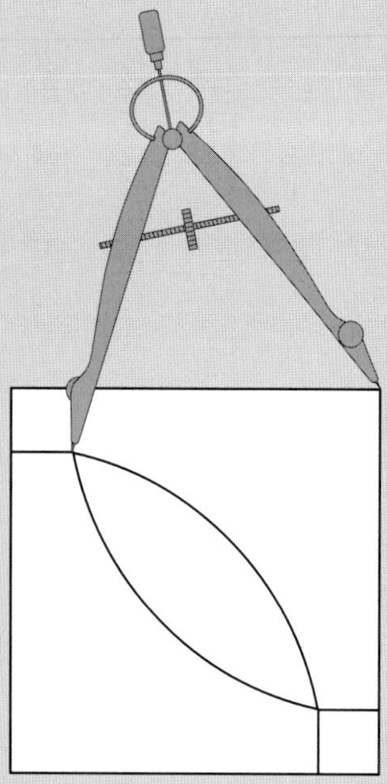

5. Evaluate the center melon shape. Does it look too small? Is it too flat? If so, erase the arcs and place the compass point 1" inside the corner of the larger square; readjust the compass and repeat the process. Now how does it look? (One inch is an arbitrary measurement. Try several locations; you are the designer.)

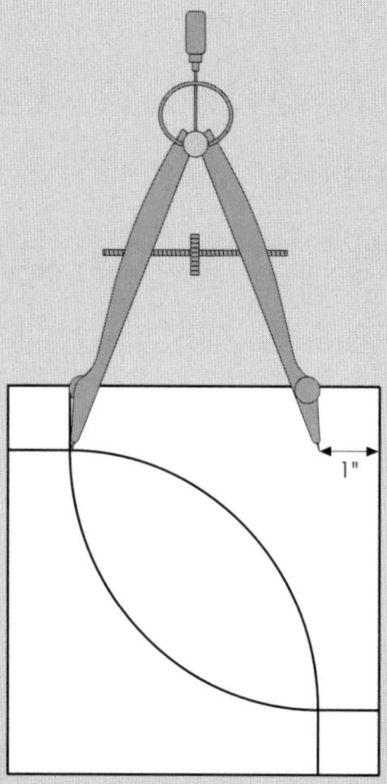

1"

When the curved design pleases you, make the following marks:

• Registration marks: Place a ruler from corner to corner of the square, crossing the melon shape. Mark the center on both edges.

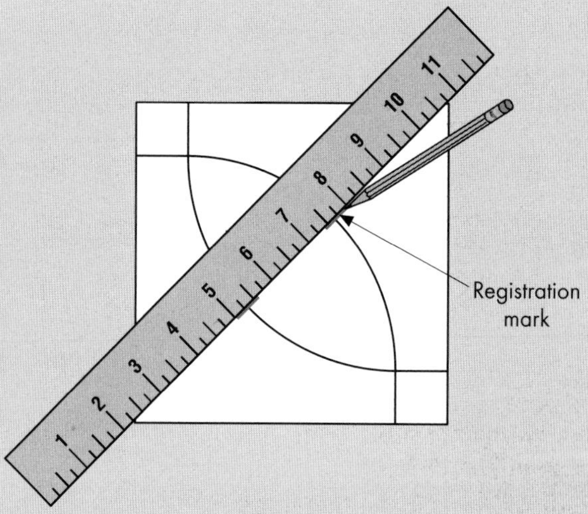

Registration mark

• Grain-line arrows: Mark these on each piece, matching the graph-paper lines.

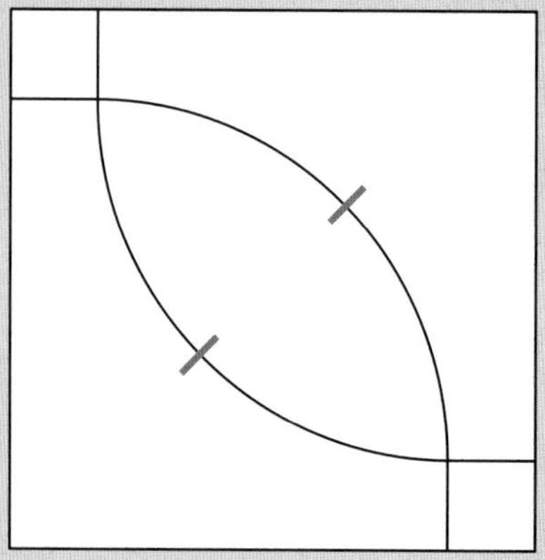

Make templates using your design. I never cut the original design but keep it for reference.

1. Trace the pattern pieces on transparent plastic. Cut on the lines. See "Templates" on pages 13–15.

2. Check the pattern's accuracy by placing the templates over the drawn design. Turn the template over and check that both sides match the pattern. The melon should be symmetrical, and the corner pieces should be interchangeable. If you are hand piecing, these are the templates you'll use.

3. For machine piecing, you need to add seam allowances to your pattern pieces. If the curve is an arc from a true circle, measure ¼" from the center registration mark. Place the compass in its original position and open it to the ¼" mark you just made on the graph paper. Using a different colored pencil, draw the arc.

4. Trace the new template, with seam allowances added. Don't forget to add seam allowances to the straight edges and to mark the registration marks and grain-line arrows on the templates.

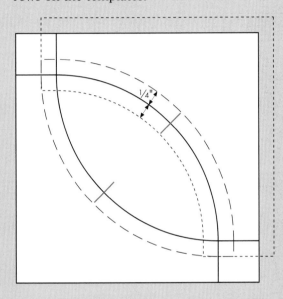

If the curve is not a true arc, add ¼" in one of the following ways:

• Use a ruler to mark ¼" at tiny increments along the curve. Connect the marks to create a seam-allowance line.

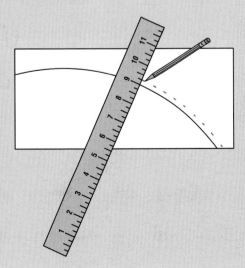

• Make a combination template and use it to mark the curved seam allowance with a rolling circle marker on another piece of template plastic. See "Tools and Supplies" on page 9.

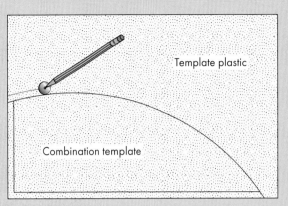

Template plastic

Combination template

Cut out the new template, with the seam allowances added. Punch holes where the seams intersect and cut registration notches.

Following are more curved patterns to draft. You decide the block size. You may need more than one square to draw the block pieces.

Drunkard's Path

1. Draw a square.

2. Place the compass point at the X and the pencil at the O. Draw an arc. In the classic Drunkard's Path block, the O is at a point approximately ¼ the length of the edge. However, you can set it at any point along the edge, depending on the size of the circle you'd like to make.

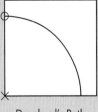

Drunkard's Path

Orange Peel

1. Draw 5 adjoining squares as shown. Draw diagonal lines through the outer squares to find the center of each square.
2. Place the compass point at the X and the pencil at the O; draw an arc. Place the O far enough from the corner of the square to avoid interfering with the seam allowances. Try moving the O to different positions, which will vary the arc. Without changing the compass setting, move the point to the remaining Xs to strike the other arcs.

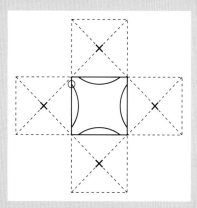

Orange Peel

Double Ax

1. Draw 3 adjoining squares as shown. Draw diagonal lines through each square to find the center.
2. Place the compass point at the X of the middle square and the pencil at the O. Draw an arc on the left and right sides. Without changing the compass setting, move the point to the upper and lower Xs to strike the remaining arcs.

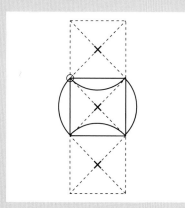

Double Ax

Using a Flexible Curve

Sometimes a compass is too confining when you want to design a curved line. A flexible curve (page 8) gives you the freedom you need.

1. Draw a square the desired size on graph paper.
2. Form a pleasing curve with the tool.
3. Use the tool to draw a smooth curve on the square. To that curve, you must add a seam allowance using a ruler or a rolling circle marker.

Most flexible curves do not have a ruler on them. I use small pieces of tape to mark the beginning and end of the curve I've shaped. Then I can turn and repeat the shape.

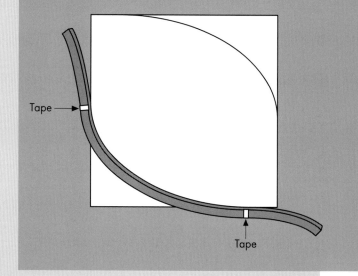

Tape

Tape

Gallery

True Lover's Knot *by Paulette Peters, 1998, Elkhorn, Nebraska,*
30" x 40". A beautiful floral print creates a painterly quality in
this two-color quilt. A flash of color accents the border.
Directions begin on page 60.

Drunkard's Path *by Paulette Peters, 1998, Elkhorn, Nebraska,
33½ " x 33½ ". Curved pieces lend a formal look to reproduction
fabrics. Although the design looks complex, all the curved units
are simple-to-sew Drunkard's Path blocks.
Directions begin on page 48.*

Sunflower *by Paulette Peters, 1998, Elkhorn, Nebraska, 17" x 28½".*
You never know where a sunflower might show up—perhaps on your wall?
Change the colors to "grow" a different flower. Directions begin on page 54.

Double Ax *by Paulette Peters, 1998, Elkhorn, Nebraska, 22" x 22".*
Hot colors add spice to the traditional Double Ax unit. It only
takes one template to create the center section of the quilt.
Directions begin on page 65.

Orange Peel *by Paulette Peters, 1998, Elkhorn, Nebraska,
35" x 35". Red and white are traditional colors for this traditional
pattern. Add a pieced border, and you create a contemporary
version of an old favorite. Directions begin on page 69.*

Four Tulips Pillow *by Paulette Peters, Elkhorn, Nebraska,*
16" x 16". Tulips with dimensional points add a springlike touch to any
room. These easy curves are a good introduction to curved piecing.
Directions begin on page 34.

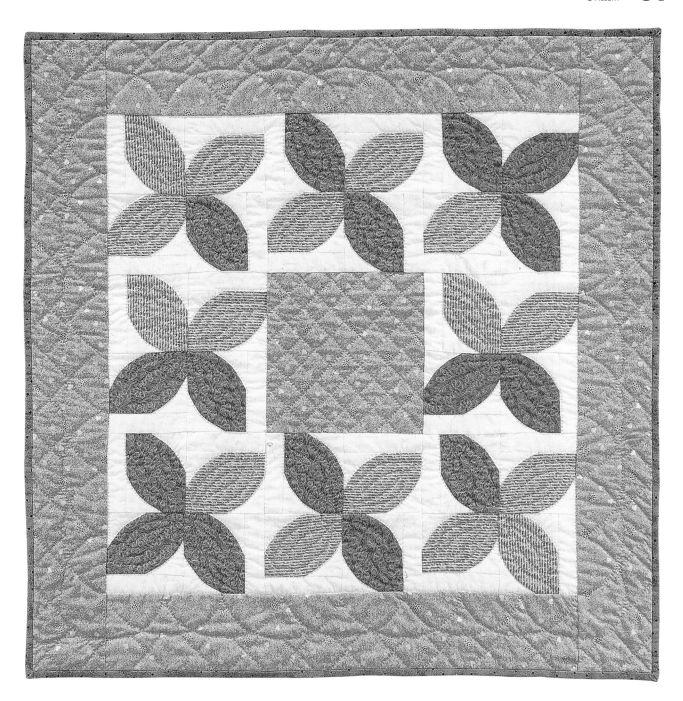

Windflowers *by Paulette Peters, 1998, Elkhorn, Nebraska, 32" x 32". Random placement of the petal fabrics creates the illusion of flowers blowing gently in the wind. Directions begin on page 74.*

Double Wedding Ring Table Runner
*by Paulette Peters, Elkhorn,
Nebraska, 18½ " x 40". This table
runner makes a great wedding
or anniversary gift.
Directions begin on page 40.*

Curved-Piecing Projects

The projects on the following pages are all relatively small, giving you the opportunity to experiment and play with curved-piecing techniques without quilting "acres and acres" of fabric. Make one or more of the projects to give to family and friends, or to yourself. Then think of creative ways to use these small pieces. Walls are good display areas. So are armchairs, sofas, tables, shelves, and balcony or stair railings.

You'll find the following information to help you make each project:
• Project information, followed by a list of materials
  • Hints for choosing fabric
  • Recommended template style
  • Cutting directions for blocks, borders, and binding
  • Directions for hand piecing and machine piecing
  • Assembly directions

Pay careful attention to the recommended template style for each project. Refer to "Template Style" on pages 13–14 for an explanation of the four kinds of templates—finished-size, cut-size, combination, and window—you can use in curved piecing. I suggest a template style for each project, but you may choose to use another.

An important reminder: On each block piece that you cut, mark the registration marks and the dots where the curved seams start and end. These marks are essential for stitching smooth curves.

If you need help with binding your quilt and adding a hanging sleeve, refer to *Your First Quilt Book*.

Ready? Set? It's time to start piecing "around the bend."

Four Tulips Pillow

A pillow is a beautiful way to practice curved piecing before tackling your first curvy quilt. This block has gentle curves, and each tulip has a folded tip, which adds dimension to the surface. It's easy and it's fun!

Color photo on page 30.

Project Information at a Glance	
Finished Pillow Size:	16" x 16"
Finished Block Size:	11" x 11"
Finished Border Width:	2½"

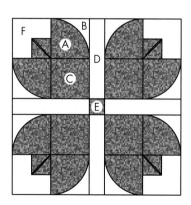

Letters identify templates.

Materials: 44"-wide fabric

¼ yd. or fat quarter blue batik for tulips

½ yd. white solid or tone-on-tone print for background and pillow-top backing

⅝ yd. yellow print for border and pillow back

2 yds. pre-gathered eyelet or lace, 2½" wide, for edging

18" x 18" square of low-loft batting

16" pillow form

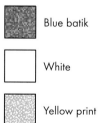

Blue batik

White

Yellow print

Choosing Fabric

When it comes to fabrics, the only limit is your imagination. Be sure there is enough contrast between the flower fabric and the background. You might like to use another fabric for the folded flower centers.

Recommended Template Style

I used combination templates to hand piece the curved units and machine piece the blocks. See "Combination template" on page 14 and "Combined Techniques" on page 19.

Cutting

All measurements include ¼"-wide seam allowances. Use the templates on page 39.

Don't forget to cut ¼" beyond to the curve when you use combination Templates A and B. This ¼" becomes the seam allowance.

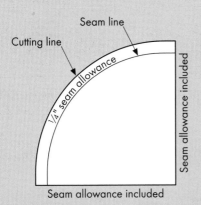

Combination Template A

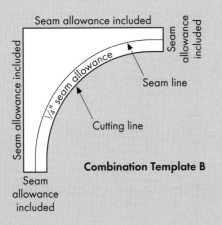

Combination Template B

From the blue batik, cut:

16 squares, each 3" x 3", for the flowers. On 8 squares, draw the convex curve for Piece A using your template. Cut the curve with scissors on the cutting line, or ¼" beyond the seam line if you are using a combination template.

1 square, 1½" x 1½", for piece E

From the white fabric, cut:

1 square, 18" x 18". Set aside to back the pillow top for quilting.
4 rectangles, each 1½" x 5½", for Piece D
4 squares, each 3" x 3", for Piece F
4 rectangles, each 3" x 4". On each rectangle, draw the concave curve for 2 Piece B using your template. Cut the curve with scissors on the cutting line, or ¼" beyond the seam line if you are using a combination template.

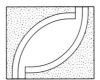

Remember to mark the registration mark and dots where the curved seam starts and ends on each piece.

From the yellow print, cut:

2 rectangles, each 14" x 16½". Set aside for the back of the pillow.
2 rectangles, each 3" x 11½", for borders
2 rectangles, each 3" x 16½", for borders

Block Assembly

1. Join Pieces A and B by hand to make a curved unit. Match the registration marks and dots where the curved seams start and end. Press the seam toward the convex side. Make 8 units. Each unit should measure 3" x 3". Block the units if necessary; see "Blocking Your Blocks" on page 20.

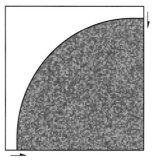

Make 8.

2. To make a folded flower center, press a 3" blue batik square diagonally from corner to corner, right side out. Fold again on each side, bringing the folded edge to the middle. Place the raw edges of the folded square on one corner of a white Piece F. Machine baste as shown. Make 4.

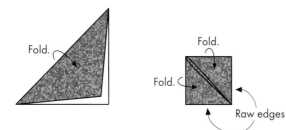

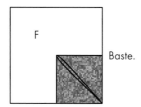

Make 4.

3. Assemble the curved units, flower-center square, and blue square as shown. Remove the basting.

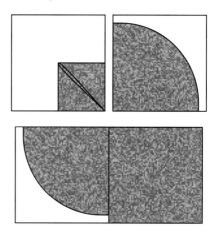

4. Assemble the tulip units, white sashing strips, and blue center square into rows. Join the rows to make the block.

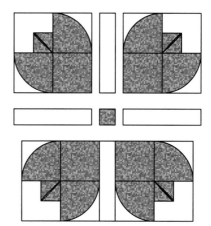

Pillow Assembly

1. Add the 3" x 11½" yellow borders to opposite sides of the pillow top. Press the seam
allowances toward the borders. Add the
3" x 16½" yellow borders to the top and
bottom of the pillow top.

2. Layer the pillow top, batting, and backing;
baste. Quilt as desired. Do not quilt the
folded flower center; it's too thick, and you
want it to remain free.
3. Baste by hand or machine ¼" from the edge
of the pillow top. Trim the excess batting
and backing.

Here's how to taper the corners so they
don't form exaggerated points:
1. On each side of the pillow top,
mark a spot 4" from the corner.
2. On each side, mark a spot ½" from the
corner.
3. Connect the marks as shown with a ruler
and pencil. Trim on the lines. When you
baste the eyelet, align the gathered edge
with the edge of the pillow top.

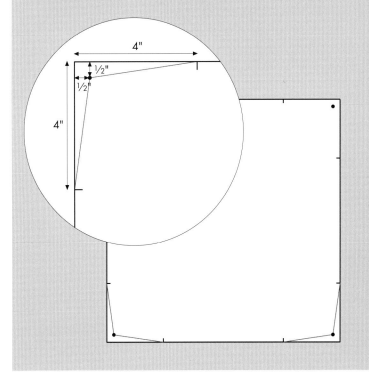

4. Baste the eyelet trim ¼" from the edges of the pillow top, leaving extra fullness at the corners.

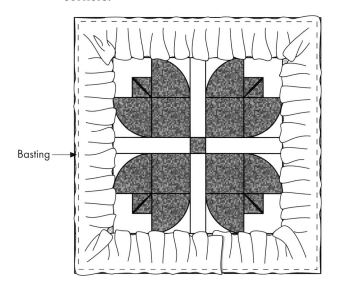

Basting →

5. Fold under 1" on the ruffle ends where they meet, to conceal the raw edges. When the pillow is finished, tack the fold in place.

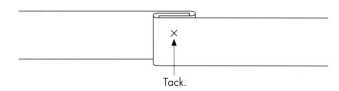

×

Tack.

 Machine baste the free edge of the ruffle to the pillow top before finishing to keep it from getting caught in the seam. Use very long stitches.

Finishing

1. Hem one 16½"-long edge of each of the backing rectangles. Turn under ¼"; then turn under another 1½". Machine stitch the edge.

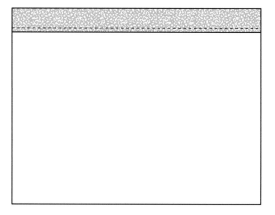

Make 2.

2. With right sides together, place one hemmed rectangle on top of the quilted pillow, matching the outside edges; pin. Baste as shown, ¼" from the edge.

Basting

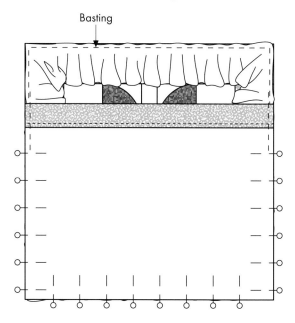

3. Place the other rectangle on top of the pillow, right sides together; pin. Sew through all layers, using a ¼"-wide seam allowance. Double-stitch where the two rectangles overlap. Trim the batting from the seam allowance. Trim the corners and turn the pillow right side out.

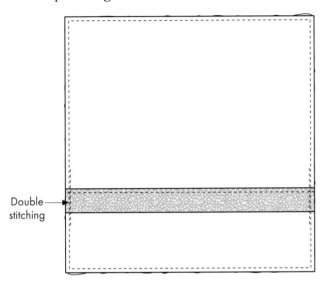

Double → stitching

4. Pop in a 16" pillow form.

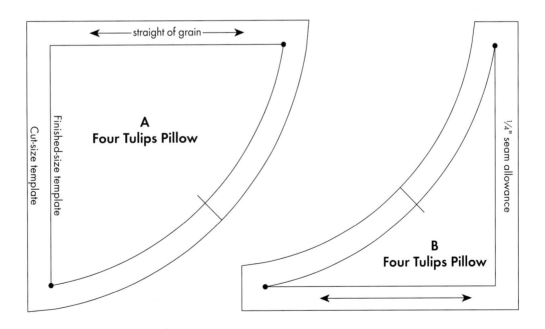

straight of grain

Cut-size template

Finished-size template

A
Four Tulips Pillow

¼" seam allowance

B
Four Tulips Pillow

Double Wedding Ring Table Runner

Double Wedding Ring, a beloved quilt pattern with a long history, is one of the most recognizable and most requested patterns in quiltmaking classes. Consider this table runner a beginning Wedding Ring quilt. It's a great place to start if you've always wanted to make this design. In the following project, edge pieces make the runner straight.

Project Information at a Glance	
Finished Size:	18½" x 40"
Finished Ring Size:	15¼" x 15¼"

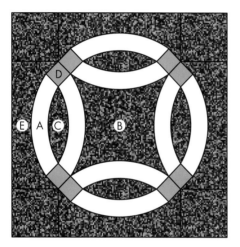

Letters identify templates.

Materials: 44"-wide fabric

⅛ yd. or fat eighth red for corner squares
⅝ yd. white for arcs
1½ yds. black print for background and lining
⅝ yd. muslin to back runner for quilting
22" x 44" piece of thin batting

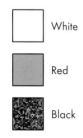

White

Red

Black

Color photo on page 32.

Choosing Fabric

A multicolored print is a good choice for the background and lining. (Using the same fabric for the background and lining makes the edges of the runner inconspicuous.) Select fabrics for the arcs and small squares that contrast with the background. You want the rings to be clearly defined.

Recommended Template Style

I suggest using cut-size templates and machine piecing for this project. See "Template Style" on page 13 and "Curved Piecing by Machine" on page 18.

Cutting

All measurements include ¼"-wide seam allowances. Use the templates on pages 45–47.

From the red fabric, cut:
    1 strip, 2" x 42". Crosscut 20 squares, each 2" x 2", or use Template D.

From the white fabric, cut:
    20 arcs using Template A

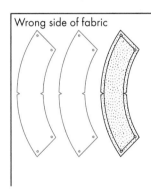

From the black fabric, cut:
    2 rectangles, each 19" x 21", for lining
    3 large centers using Template B

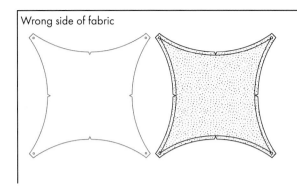

10 melon shapes using Template C

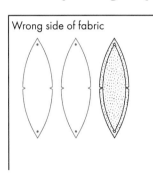

8 rectangles, each 5" x 11⅛". Use Template E to draw the curved edge. Cut the curve with scissors.

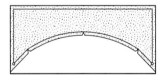

4 squares, each 4½" x 4½", for corners

For Templates A, B, C, and E, align the grain-line arrow with the straight grain of the fabric. Mark the registration marks and the dots where the curved seams start and end.

Table Runner Assembly

1. Sew an arc (Piece A) to one side of each melon shape (Piece C). Press the seam toward the arc. You will need to clip the concave seam allowance to allow it to lie flat. See "Pressing Curved Seams" on page 20.

2. Sew a square (Piece D) to each end of each remaining arc. Press the seams toward the arcs.

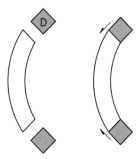

3. Join the units made in steps 1 and 2, matching the registration marks and the dots where the curved seams start and end. Press the seams toward the arcs. Make 10 melon units.

Make 10.

4. Sew a melon unit to opposite sides of one center piece (Piece B). Sew a melon unit to each of the remaining sides to make a complete ring.

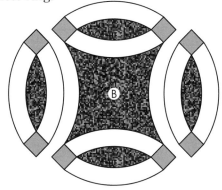

Make 1.

5. Sew a melon unit to opposite sides of each remaining center piece. Sew a melon unit to one side of each center piece.

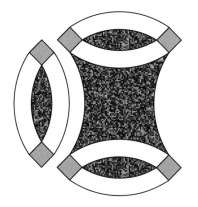

Make 2.

6. Join the units, matching the registration marks and dots where the curved seams start and end.

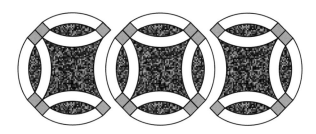

Backstitch at the start and end of each seam, leaving the seam allowances free.

7. Sew 3 edge pieces (Piece E) to one long side of the rings. Pin at the centers and dots where the curved seams start and end. Stitch, backstitching at the start and end of each seam. (Do not cross the seam allowances.) Leave the straight seams open.

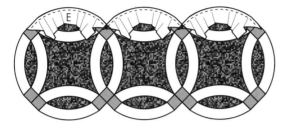

Repeat on the opposite long side.

8. To complete the straight seams, fold the table runner right sides together as shown. Pin the dot where the straight seam meets the curved seam. Stitch the seam, stopping at the pin; backstitch.

Stitch from edge to pin.

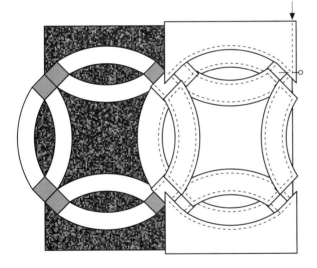

9. Sew a corner square to each end of the 2 remaining edge pieces, stopping at the dots.

10. Sew the units made in the previous step to the ends of the ring unit along the curved seams, stopping at the dots.

11. Finish the straight seams as in step 8.

Finishing

The table runner will lie flatter without a binding. Here's how to finish your runner with an "envelope" lining.

1. Layer the muslin backing, batting, and runner top; baste.
2. Quilt by hand or machine.
3. Machine baste ¼" from the edge of the quilted top. Trim the batting and muslin even with the runner top.
4. Press under ¼" on one short edge of one lining piece. Lay the piece right side down on the runner. Pin.

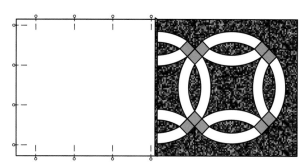

5. Lay the second piece of lining, right side down, on the runner, overlapping the pressed edge. Pin. Sew around the edges, using a walking foot and a ¼"-wide seam allowance. Trim the corners.

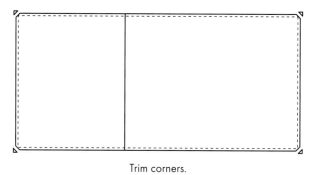

Trim corners.

6. Turn the runner right side out and push out the seams and corners. Lightly press the edges. Hand stitch the pressed edge of the lining.
7. Machine or hand quilt through all layers ½" from the edge.

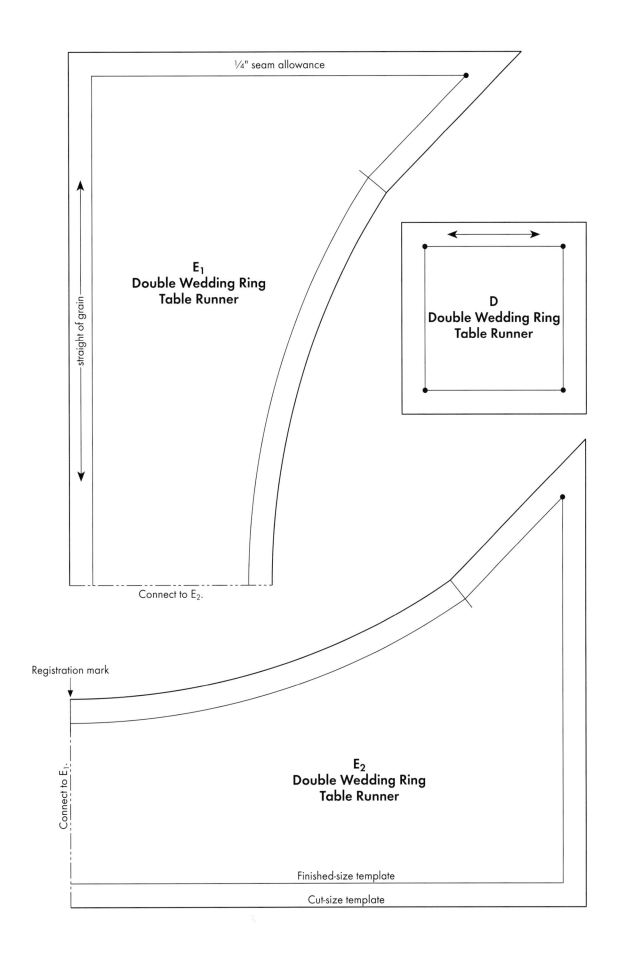

¼" seam allowance

E₁
**Double Wedding Ring
Table Runner**

straight of grain

Connect to E₂.

D
**Double Wedding Ring
Table Runner**

Registration mark

Connect to E₁.

E₂
**Double Wedding Ring
Table Runner**

Finished-size template

Cut-size template

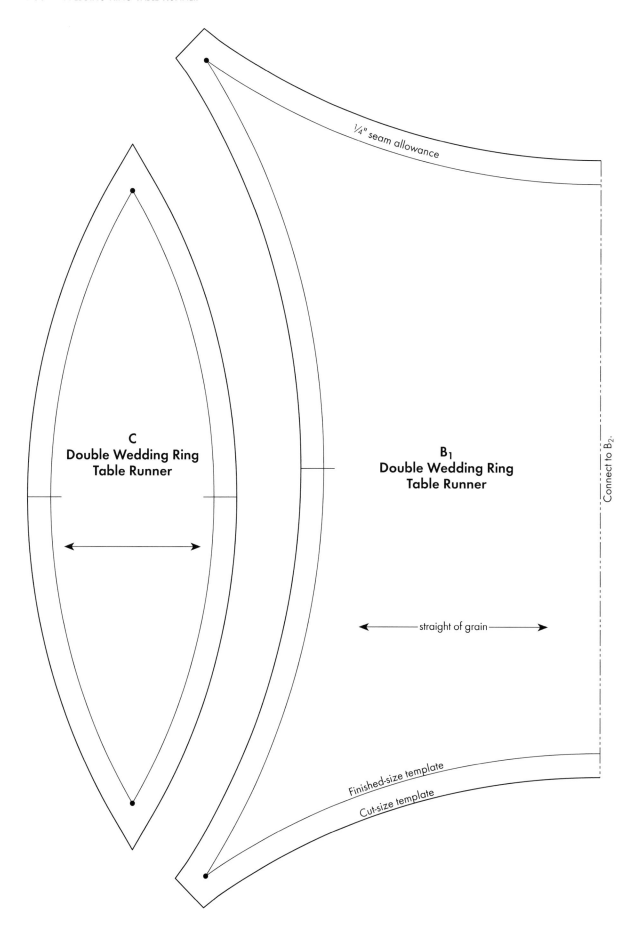

¼" seam allowance

C
Double Wedding Ring
Table Runner

B₁
Double Wedding Ring
Table Runner

straight of grain

Finished-size template

Cut-size template

Connect to B₂.

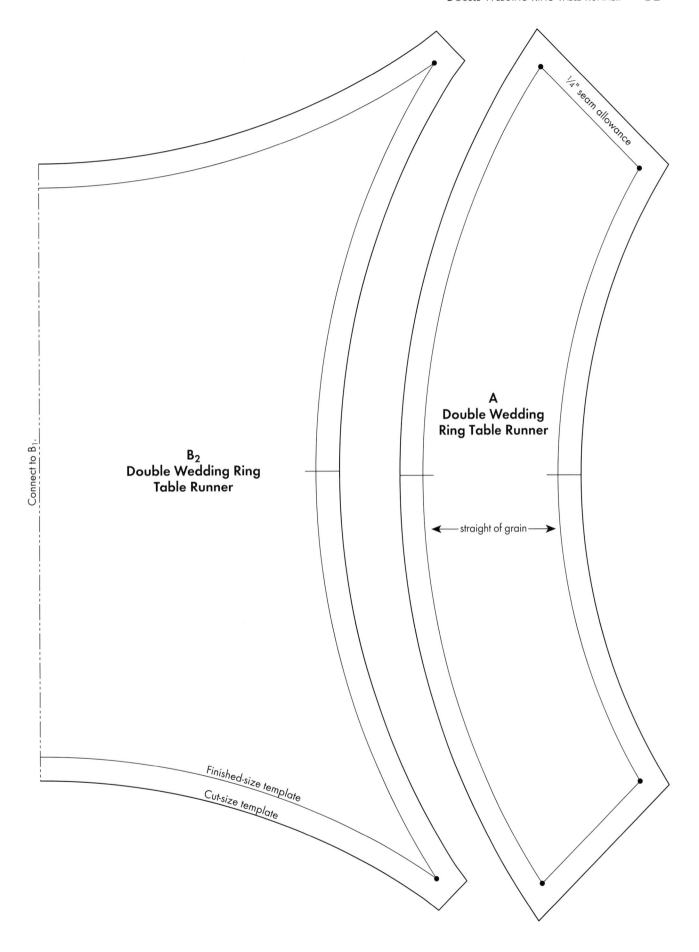

Connect to B₁.

B₂
Double Wedding Ring
Table Runner

Finished-size template

Cut-size template

¼" seam allowance

A
Double Wedding
Ring Table Runner

← straight of grain →

Drunkard's Path

A classic, this block is the basic curved-piecing pattern. The unit is very versatile—twist and turn it for many different designs and settings. This setting is known as "Love Ring," and you have two options for borders. If you love making these blocks—and they are fun—make twelve more and turn them on point for a fancy, on-point border that only looks complex. If you're in a hurry, make only four more blocks for the corners of a simple border.

On-point border

Color photo on page 26.

Project Information at a Glance

Finished Quilt Size:	33½" x 33½"
With On-Point Border	33½" x 33½"
With Simple Border	30" x 30"
Finished Block Size:	5" x 5"
Finished On-Point Border Width:	6¾"
Finished Simple Border Width:	5"

Letters identify templates.

Simple border

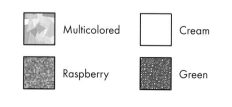

Multicolored Cream

Raspberry Green

Materials: 44"-wide fabric

½ yd. multicolored floral print for blocks and either border

⅜ yd. raspberry for blocks and border inset

¾ yd. cream for blocks and on-point border **or** ½ yd. cream for blocks and simple border

1⅛ yds. green for on-point border and binding **or** ⅝ yd. green for simple border and binding

1⅛ yds. for backing

38" x 38" piece of batting

Choosing Fabric

This project gives you the opportunity to use elegant, formal fabrics. Civil War–era reproduction fabrics that reflect a genteel lifestyle work nicely with the curved design lines. In the large background areas, I used a lively cream print. You might select a plain fabric or an elegant white-on-white to show off your quilting stitches in those areas. The center medallion area has four intersecting seam lines. Choose a large-scale, multicolored print to help camouflage the seams.

You have two options for the border. Read through the directions for the on-point border and simple border before making your decision.

Recommended Template Style

The curve in this block is a true quarter circle. It is the deepest curve in this book, but it is large enough to allow easy machine piecing. I used cut-size templates and pieced the units by machine. See "Template Style" on page 13 and "Curved Piecing by Machine" on page 18.

Cutting

All measurements include ¼"-wide seam allowances. Use the templates on page 53.

 Remember to mark the registration marks in the seam allowances and dots where the curved seams start and end.

From the multicolored fabric, cut:
  2 rectangles, each 5½" x 7½". Use Template A to mark the curved edges. Cut 2 pieces from each rectangle with scissors to make 4.

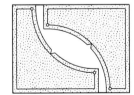

From the raspberry fabric, cut:
  4 strips, each 1" x 20½", for border inset
  12 squares, each 4½" x 4½". Use Template B to mark the curved edges. Cut with scissors.

From the cream fabric, cut:
  4 rectangles, each 5½" x 7½". Use Template A to mark the curved edges. Cut 2 pieces from each rectangle with scissors to make 8.
  4 squares, each 5½" x 5½", for corners

Block Assembly

1. Start by making Block A. To begin the seam, place multicolored Piece A, wrong side up, on top of raspberry Piece B, aligning the straight edges. Pin.

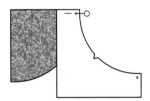

2. Take 2 or 3 stitches; stop with the needle down. Bring the raw edges into alignment and take a few more stitches; stop with the needle down. Bring the raw edges into alignment and pin the pieces together at the registration marks. Continue to sew slowly, aligning the raw edges every few stitches.

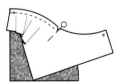

3. Move the pin to the end of the seam, and continue sewing a few stitches at a time.

4. Press the seam allowances toward the convex (raspberry) side. See "Pressing Curved Seams" on page 20. Your blocks should measure 5½" x 5½". Block if necessary; see "Blocking Your Blocks" on page 20. Make 4 of Block A.

Block A
Make 4.

5. Using raspberry Piece B and cream Piece A, make 8 of Block B. Press the seam allowances toward the convex (raspberry) side.

Block B
Make 8.

Quilt Assembly

Arrange the blocks in rows, with a plain square in each corner. Sew the blocks together in groups of 4. Join the groups to make the center section of the quilt.

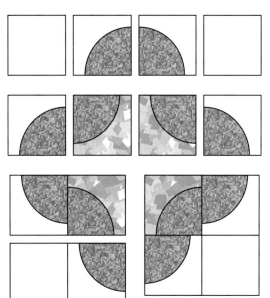

Border Inset

Add a flash of color with a border inset.

1. Fold each strip lengthwise, wrong sides together, and press firmly.

1"

Fold

2. Using a ⅛"-wide seam allowance, sew a folded strip to opposite sides of the quilt top, matching the raw edges.

3. Sew a strip to the top and bottom edges, overlapping the first strips at the corners. Add the border of your choice, using ¼"-wide seam allowances. The folded edge will peek out ¼".

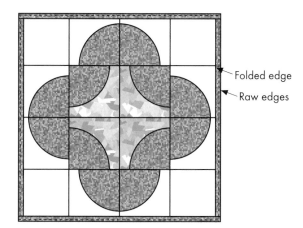

Folded edge

Raw edges

On-Point Border

Make this impressive border to frame the center of the quilt.

Cutting

Use the templates on page 53.

From the green fabric, cut:
    6 rectangles, each 5½" x 7½". Use Template A to mark the curved edges. Cut 2 pieces from each rectangle with scissors to make 12.
    2 squares, each 8" x 8". Cut each square twice diagonally to make 8 side setting triangles (Piece C).

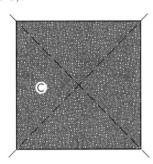

    4 squares, each 4¼" x 4¼". Cut each square once diagonally to make 8 corner setting triangles (Piece D).

    4 squares, each 7¼" x 7¼", for corners
    4 strips, each 2½" x 42", for binding

From the cream fabric, cut:
    12 squares, each 5½" x 5½". Use Template B to mark the curved edge. Cut with scissors.

From the multicolored print, cut:
    2 squares, each 8" x 8". Cut each square twice diagonally to make 8 side setting triangles (Piece C).
    4 squares, each 4¼" x 4¼". Cut each square once diagonally to make 8 corner setting triangles (Piece D).

Border Assembly

1. Make the cream and green blocks as you did the center blocks. On the green edges of each block, trim ¼" so the block measures 5¼" x 5¼". (Each block needs to be smaller to fit along the edge of your quilt.)

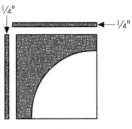

Make 12.

2. Join the blocks, multicolored C triangles, and green C triangles into diagonal rows. Join the rows. Add the D triangles last.

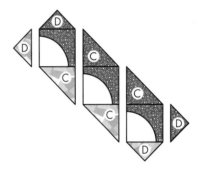

3. Add a pieced border to each side of the quilt top. Add a 7¼" green square to each end of each remaining pieced border. Add the borders to the top and bottom of the quilt top. Trim the corners if necessary.

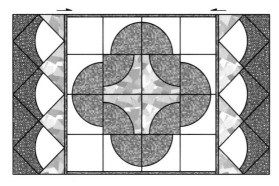

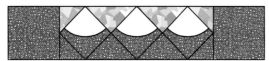

Simple Border

Make this easy border if you're pressed for time or want a simple frame for your quilt.

Cutting

Use the templates on page 53.

From the green fabric, cut:
 2 rectangles, each 5½" x 7½". Use Template A to mark the curved edges. Cut 2 pieces from each rectangle with scissors to make 4.
 4 strips, each 1½" x 20½"
 4 strips, each 2½" x 42", for binding

From the multicolored fabric, cut:
 4 squares, each 5½" x 5½". Use Template B to mark the curved edges. Cut with scissors.
 4 strips, each 4½" x 20½"

Block Assembly

Assemble four corner blocks as you did for the center of the quilt.

Border Assembly

1. Join a green and a multicolored border strip. Press the seam allowances toward the green strip. Make 4.

Make 4.

2. Add a pieced border strip to opposite sides of the quilt top. Add a corner block to each end of each remaining pieced border strip. Add the borders to the top and bottom of the quilt top.

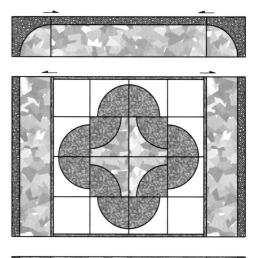

Finishing

1. Layer the quilt top with backing and batting; baste.
2. Quilt by hand or machine.
3. Bind the edges with the green strips.
4. Add a label to your finished quilt.

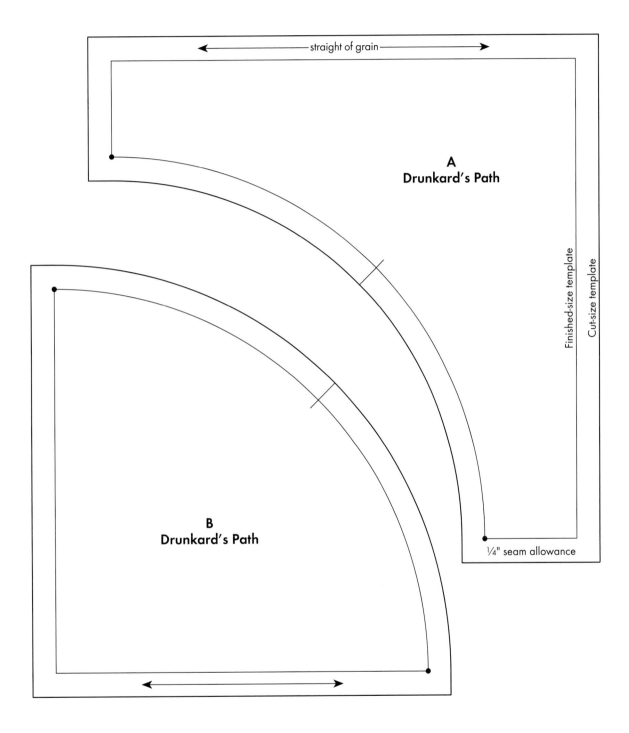

straight of grain

A
Drunkard's Path

Finished-size template

Cut-size template

¼" seam allowance

B
Drunkard's Path

Sunflower

Easy curves and simple piecing combine to make a flower that appears to blow gently in the wind. Mine is a sunflower. You might like to make yours a daisy or a child's pinwheel.

Project Information at a Glance	
Finished Quilt Size:	17" x 28½"
Finished Block Size:	12" x 12"
Finished Border Width:	2½"

Letters identify templates.

Color photo on page 27.

Materials: 44"-wide fabric

½ yd. yellow print for background
⅜ yd. gold batik for petals
Scrap (4" x 4") of dark brown for flower center
¼ yd. or fat quarter dark green for leaves
　　and stem
¼ yd. multicolored print for border
⅜ yd. rust batik for corners and binding
⅝ yd. fabric for backing
22" x 32" piece of batting

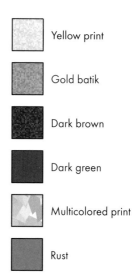

Yellow print

Gold batik

Dark brown

Dark green

Multicolored print

Rust

Choosing Fabric

Because half of the flower petals are cut on the straight grain and half on the bias, it's best to avoid geometric prints and plaids for these pieces. Make sure there is good contrast between the background fabric and the flower and its leaves.

Recommended Template Style

I used combination templates to piece the curves by hand and the straight lines by machine. See "Combination template" on page 14 and "Combined Techniques" on page 19.

 The petals are directional. The templates have already been reversed for you. Use them on the wrong side of the fabric, with the printed side of the template up. Your flower will blow in the same direction as mine. If you want the wind to come from the other direction, turn the templates over.

Cutting

All measurements include ¼"-wide seam allowances. Use the templates on pages 58–59.

Remember to mark the registration marks in the seam allowances and dots where the curved seams start and end.

From the yellow print, cut:

1 strip, 6⅞" x 42". Crosscut 2 squares, each 6¼" x 6¼". Set aside for "Leaves and Stem," step 2.

Crosscut 4 squares, each 6⅞" x 6⅞". Cut each square once diagonally to make 8 triangles.

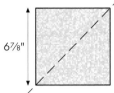

4 Piece A, using your template and the triangles just cut. Align the edges of the template with the straight edges of the triangle and draw the curved seam.

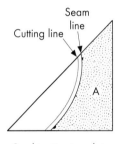

Combination template

For a combination template, remember to cut the curved seam ¼" beyond the drawn line.

4 Piece B as above, from the remaining triangles.

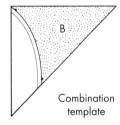

Combination template

2 squares, each 6½" x 6½". From each square, cut 2 Piece E.

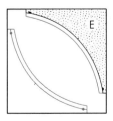

Combination template

From the gold batik, cut:
  1 strip, 5¼" x 42". Cut 4 Piece C petals with the short side on the straight grain and the long side on the bias grain.

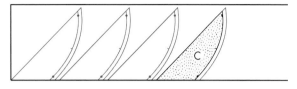

Combination template

Sew each Piece C to a Piece A. Press the seams toward the petals.

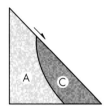

  1 strip, 2½" x 42". Cut 4 Piece C petals with the spine on the straight grain.

Combination template

Sew each Piece C to a Piece B. Press the seams toward the petals.

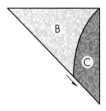

From the brown fabric, cut:
  4 squares, each 1¾" x 1¾", for flower center

From the green fabric, cut:
  1 strip, 1" x 12", for the stem
  2 squares, each 6¼" x 6¼". Draw the curved seams, using Template D.

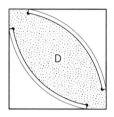

Combination template

From the multicolored print, cut:
  2 strips, each 3" x 24", for side borders
  2 strips, each 3" x 12½", for top and bottom borders

From the rust batik, cut:
  4 squares, each 3" x 3", for border corners
  3 strips, each 2½" x 42", for binding

Assembly

Flower

1. Join an A and a B triangle/petal unit to make a flower square. The square should measure 6½" x 6½". Block, if necessary; see "Blocking Your Blocks" on page 20. Make 4.

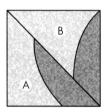

Make 4.

2. For the flower center, fold a brown square diagonally and press. Align the square with the inner corner of the flower square, right sides together. Sew on the fold. Trim the excess fabric underneath to ¼". Repeat with the remaining flower squares.

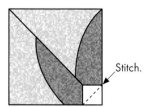

Stitch.

Press the seams of two flower centers toward the center, and two toward the petals to make it easier to interlock the seams.

3. Join 4 flower squares to make the flower, matching the seams at the center.

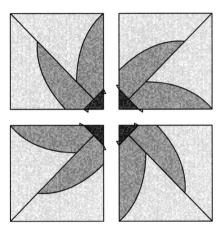

Leaves and Stem
1. Sew a yellow Piece E to each curve of a green Piece D, matching the registration marks and the dots where the curved seams start and end. Make 2.

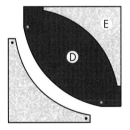

Make 2.

2. Sew a 6¼" yellow square to the top of each leaf unit. Join the units with the stem in between.

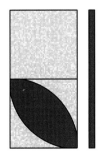

3. Join the flower to the leaf/stem unit.

Borders
Add the 3" x 24" multicolored border strips to the sides of the quilt top. Add a 3" rust batik square to each end of each 3" x 12½" multicolored border strip. Add the borders to the top and bottom of the quilt top.

Finishing
1. Layer the quilt top with batting and backing; baste.
2. Quilt by hand or machine. I quilted in-the-ditch around each piece.
3. Bind the edges with the rust strips.
4. Add a label to your finished wall quilt.

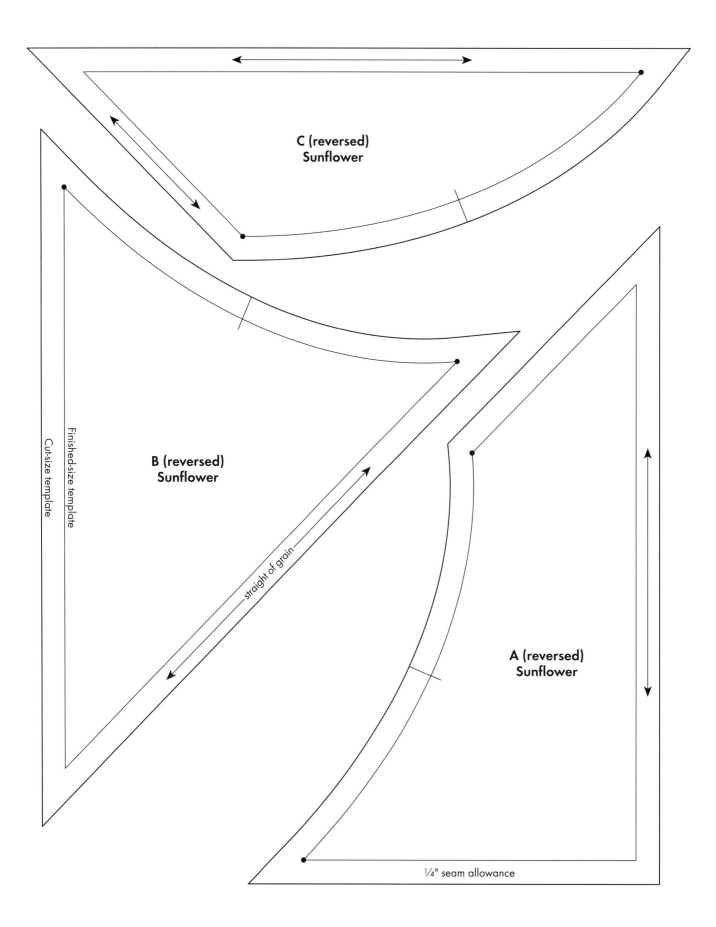

C (reversed)
Sunflower

B (reversed)
Sunflower

A (reversed)
Sunflower

Cut-size template

Finished-size template

straight of grain

¼" seam allowance

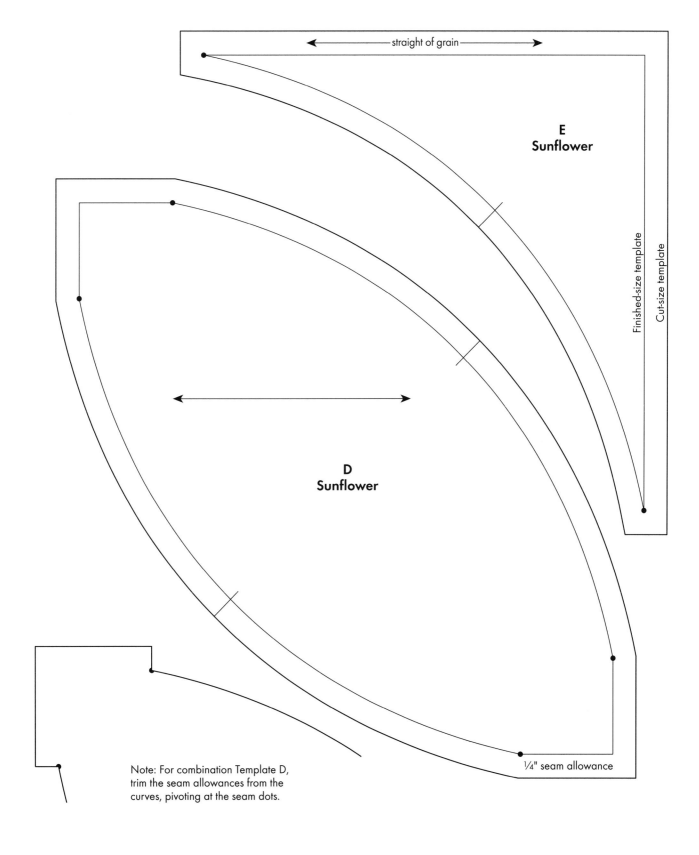

straight of grain

E
Sunflower

Finished-size template

Cut-size template

D
Sunflower

¼" seam allowance

Note: For combination Template D,
trim the seam allowances from the
curves, pivoting at the seam dots.

True Lover's Knot

A great design for a wedding gift, this pattern is traditionally stitched in two colors. Reversing the colors in some of the blocks adds interest, but all the blocks are constructed alike. The piecing is easy, the effect complex.

Color photo on page 25.

Project Information at a Glance	
Finished Quilt Size:	30" x 30"
Finished Block Size:	5" x 5"
Finished Inner Border Width:	1"
Finished Outer Border Width:	4"

Materials: 44"-wide fabric

1 ⅛ yds. dark floral print for blocks, outer border, and binding

½ yd. light print for blocks and corner squares

¼ yd. or fat quarter accent fabric for inner border and corner squares

1 yd. for backing

34" x 34" piece of batting

Letters identify templates.

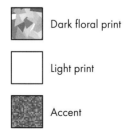

Dark floral print

Light print

Accent

Choosing Fabric

High contrast between light and dark fabrics is essential for defining the curved design in this simple quilt. Add an accent color in the inner border for visual interest.

Recommended Template Style

I used cut-size templates and machine pieced the entire quilt. See "Template Style" on page 13 and "Curved Piecing by Machine" on page 18.

Cutting

All measurements include ¼"-wide seam allowances. Use the templates on page 64.

 Remember to mark the registration marks in the seam allowances and dots where the curved seams start and end.

Block A
Make 4.

Block B
Make 12.

Block C
Make 4.

Cut the following as directed below:
Piece A—16 dark and 24 light
Piece B—12 dark and 8 light
Piece C—28 dark, 8 light, and 4 accent

From the dark fabric, cut:
2 strips, each 4½" x 42". Crosscut 8 rectangles, each 4½" x 6½". Use Template A to mark the curved edges. From each rectangle, cut 2 pieces. Cut the curves with scissors to make 16.

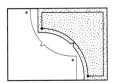

2 strips, each 3½" x 42". Use Template B to mark 12 pieces. Align the grain-line arrow. Cut the curves with scissors.

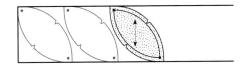

2 strips, each 1½" x 42". Crosscut 28 squares, each 1½" x 1½", for Piece C.
2 strips, each 4½" x 42", for pieced borders
3 strips, each 2½" x 42", for binding

From the light fabric, cut:
2 strips, each 4½" x 42". Crosscut 12 rectangles, each 4½" x 6½". Use Template A to mark the curved edges. Cut 2 pieces from each rectangle. Cut the curves with scissors to make 24.
1 strip, 3½" x 42". Use Template B to cut 8 pieces. Align the grain-line arrow. Cut the curves with scissors.
8 squares, each 1½" x 1½", for Piece C

From the accent fabric, cut:
2 strips, each 1½" x 42", for pieced border
4 squares, each 1½" x 1½", for Piece C

Block Assembly

Block A

Sew a dark Piece A to one side of a light Piece B, matching the registration marks and the dots where the curved seam starts and ends. Sew a light Piece C to each end of a dark Piece A. Sew the long curved seam. Make 4.

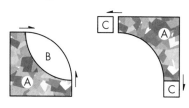

Block A
Make 4.

Each block should measure 5½" x 5½". Block if necessary; see "Blocking Your Blocks" on page 20.

Block B

Follow the directions above, reversing the colors. Make 12.

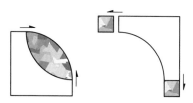

Block B
Make 12.

Block C

Sew a dark Piece A to one side of a light Piece B, matching the registration marks and the dots where the curved seam starts and ends. Sew a dark Piece C and an accent Piece C to each end of a dark Piece A. Sew the long curved seam. Make 4.

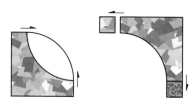

Block C
Make 4.

Quilt Assembly

1. Arrange the blocks in groups of 4 as shown; join the blocks into units. Join the units.

2. Join a dark border strip and an accent border strip. Make 2 strip sets.

3. Measure the quilt top through the center and trim 4 pieced border strips to the correct length.

Borders
Cut 4.

4. Sew a pieced border to opposite sides of the quilt top. Sew a border corner (Block C) to each end of each remaining pieced border, with the accent fabric toward the center. Sew the borders with corner blocks to the top and bottom of the quilt top.

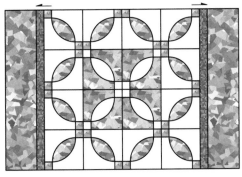

Finishing

1. Layer the quilt top with batting and backing; baste.

2. Quilt by hand or machine. I quilted in-the-ditch around each piece and used a finished-size Template B to mark the quilting design in the border.

3. Bind the edges with the dark fabric strips.

4. Add a label to your finished quilt.

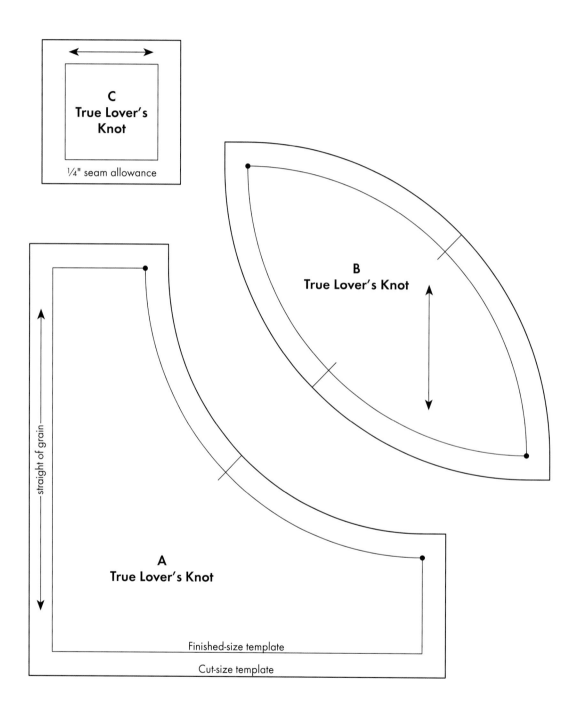

C
**True Lover's
Knot**

¼" seam allowance

B
True Lover's Knot

straight of grain

A
True Lover's Knot

Finished-size template

Cut-size template

Double Ax

It takes only one template to make this exciting quilt. The pattern has many names, including "Double Ax" and "Spools." The on-point setting creates an interesting directional design.

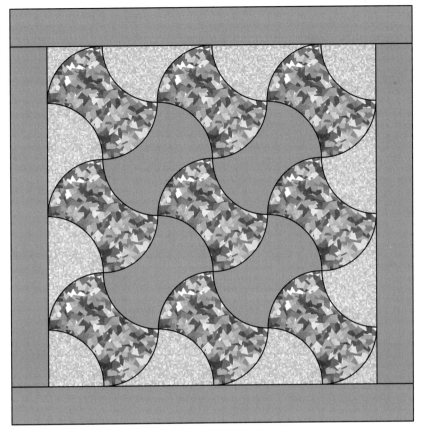

Color photo on page 28.

Project Information at a Glance	
Finished Quilt Size:	22" x 22"
Double Ax Finished Size:	6"
Finished Border Width:	2"

Materials: 44"-wide fabric

¾ yd. multicolored bright print for axes and binding

½ yd. red tone-on-tone for axes and border

½ yd. yellow tone-on-tone for axes

¾ yd. neutral print or muslin for backing

 Multicolored bright print

Red tone-on-tone

 Yellow tone-on-tone

Choosing Fabric

Traditionally this pattern has been used for charm quilts, with every piece cut from a different fabric, or scrap quilts, alternating lights and darks of many fabrics. It has a light-hearted look when you use only three colors, and it's fun to go wild with brights. Mine was hot enough to remind me of salsa.

Recommended Template Style

Machine piecing is possible, but difficult. I used a finished-size template to mark the seam lines, then added the seam allowances with a window template and hand pieced the quilt. It was fun and portable.

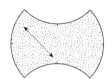

Finished-size template
for hand piecing

Window template
for hand piecing

Cutting

All measurements include ¼"-wide seam allowances. Use the template on page 68.

 Remember to mark the registration marks in the seam allowances and dots where the curved seams start and end.

From the multicolored print, cut:
3 strips, each 2½" x 42", for binding

From the red fabric, cut:
2 strips, each 2½" x 42", for borders

Using your templates, draw and cut with scissors the following pieces:
9 multicolored axes
4 red axes
12 yellow axes

Grain line is very important because every edge of the template is a curve. If you orient the template as shown below, the partial yellow axes at the edges of the quilt top will be on the straight grain, and the quilt top will lie flat for the borders.

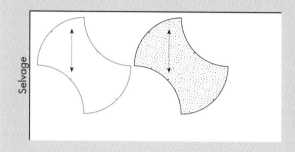

Selvage

Quilt Assembly

1. Sew the pieces into diagonal rows as shown, matching the registration marks and the dots where the curved seams start and end. Stop at each dot and do not sew across the seam allowances.

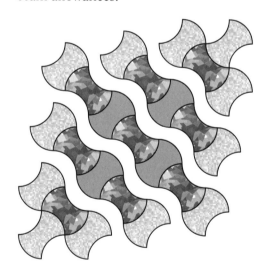

2. Sew the rows together, pinning and sewing only 1 curve at a time.

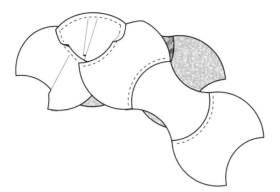

3. Press the seam allowances toward the convex side of each curve. On a long S-shaped seam, the seam allowances will alternate.

Trimming the Quilt Edges

On the wrong side of the quilt top, measure ¼" from the intersections of the ax pieces and draw straight lines for cutting. Double-check that the corners are square and that there is a ¼"-wide seam allowance beyond the stitching. Trim to make a straight edge. See why the grain line was so important?

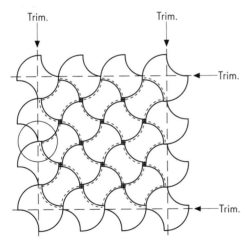

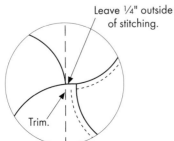

Leave ¼" outside of stitching.

Borders

1. Measure the quilt top lengthwise through the center and trim 2 border strips to this measurement. Sew the strips to opposite sides of the quilt top.

2. Measure the quilt top crosswise, including the borders you just added. Cut 2 border strips to this measurement. Sew the strips to the top and bottom of the quilt top.

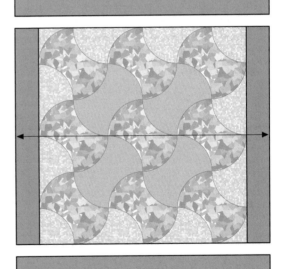

Finishing

1. Layer the quilt top with batting and backing; baste.
2. Quilt by hand or machine. I suggest quilting around each shape in-the-ditch. If you used a multicolored print, try machine quilting with variegated thread.
3. Bind the edges with the multicolored strips.
4. Add a label to your finished quilt.

Draft your own Double Ax for a larger or smaller quilt. The 6" piece in this quilt is based on a 4¼" x 4¼" square. A 3½" x 3½" square yields a 5" Double Ax. Begin by drawing 3 adjoining squares.

1. Set the compass point at the center of the middle square. Set the pencil at the corner. Draw 2 arcs on opposite sides of the square.
2. Set the compass point at the center of the square below and strike an arc into the middle square.
3. Set the compass point at the center of the square above and strike an arc into the middle square to complete the shape.

4. This shape is the finished size. Set the pencil ¼" from the arc to add seam allowances.

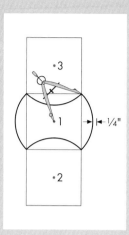

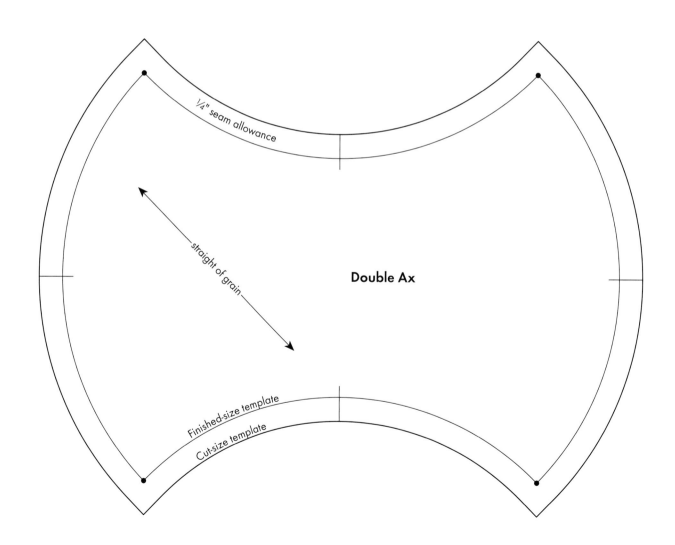

¼" seam allowance

straight of grain

Double Ax

Finished-size template

Cut-size template

Orange Peel

A striking traditional pattern, Orange Peel shows its curves best when there is high contrast between the fabrics. When the pattern is done in two colors, it's called "Rob Peter to Pay Paul." A pieced border frames the blocks and finishes the design. You can make the border blocks quickly with only one curved seam.

Color photo on page 29.

Project Information at a Glance	
Finished Quilt Size:	35" x 35"
Finished Block Size:	7" x 7"
Number of Blocks:	9
Number of Border Blocks:	12

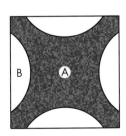

Letters identify templates.

Materials: 44"-wide fabric

2⅛ yds. white tone-on-tone or muslin for blocks and backing

1½ yds. red print for blocks and binding

39" x 39" piece of batting

White

Red

Choosing Fabric

This one is easy—only two colors—but you might want to add interest by using several different reds. If you use four reds, you will need ⅓ yard of each, plus an extra ⅓ yard of one red fabric for the binding.

Recommended Template Style

This quilt is perfect for using cut-size templates and practicing machine piecing. The curves are gentle, and there are many straight lines. The block is large enough to handle easily. See "Template Style" on page 13 and "Curved Piecing by Machine" on page 18.

Cutting

All measurements include ¼"-wide seam allowances. Use the templates on page 73.

 Remember to mark the registration marks in the seam allowances and dots where the curved seams start and end.

Note: If you are using more than one red fabric, refer to the photo on page 29 for the number of each piece to cut and the placement of the reds. The following directions are for using only one red fabric.

From the red fabric, cut:
  2 strips, each 7½" x 42". Crosscut 9 squares, each 7½" x 7½". Set 4 squares aside for the border corners. Use Template A to mark the curved edges on 5 squares. Cut the curves with scissors.
  5 strips, each 4" x 42". Set 3 strips aside for the border blocks. Crosscut 2 strips into 12 rectangles, each 4" x 6". Use Template B to mark 2 pieces on each rectangle. Cut with scissors to make 24.
  4 strips, each 2½" x 42", for binding

From the white fabric, cut:
  1 strip, 7½" x 42". Crosscut 4 squares, each 7½" x 7½". Use Template A to mark the curved edges. Cut with scissors.

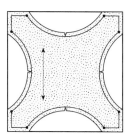

5 strips, each 4" x 42". Set 3 strips aside for the border blocks. Crosscut 2 strips into 12 rectangles, each 4" x 6". Use Template B to mark 2 pieces on each rectangle. Cut with scissors to make 24.

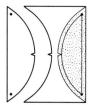

Assembly

Place Piece A on top of Piece B, right sides together. Pin the dots at one corner. Begin the seam at the edge of the fabric. Swing piece A into alignment with piece B, a few stitches at a time. As you near the center mark, pin the pieces, matching the registration marks. As you approach the end of the seam, pin the corner dots and continue sewing through the seam allowances.

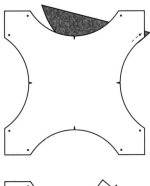

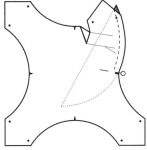

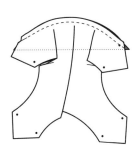

Block A

Sew a red "peel" to each side of each white Piece A. Make 4. These can be chain pieced. If you are using more than one red fabric, refer to the photo for the placement of the reds.

Block A
Make 4.

Block B

Sew a white peel to each side of each red Piece A. Make 5.

Block B
Make 4.

Border Blocks

1. Join a 4" white strip and a 4" red strip. Make 3. Crosscut the strips into 12 squares, each 7½" x 7½".

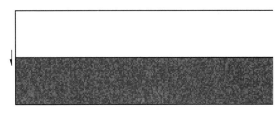

Make 3.

Cut 12 squares.

2. Use Template A to draw a curved seam on the white edge of 8 squares. Use Template A to draw a curved seam on the red edge of 4 squares. Cut the curves with scissors.

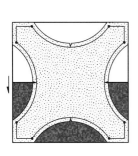

Cut one curve.

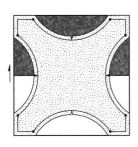

Make 8.

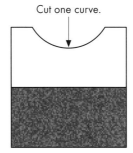

Cut one curve.

Make 4.

3. Sew a red peel to each white side. Sew a white peel to each red side. Press the seam allowances toward the red side, clipping the concave side if necessary. See "Pressing Curved Seams" on page 20.

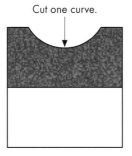

Make 8.

Make 4.

4. Join the blocks into rows. Join the rows.

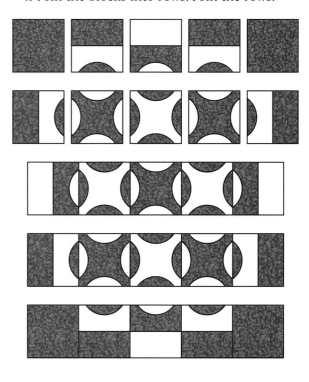

Finishing

1. Layer the quilt top with batting and backing; baste.

2. Quilt by hand or machine. See the quilting suggestion below.

3. Bind the edges with the red strips.

4. Add a label to your finished quilt.

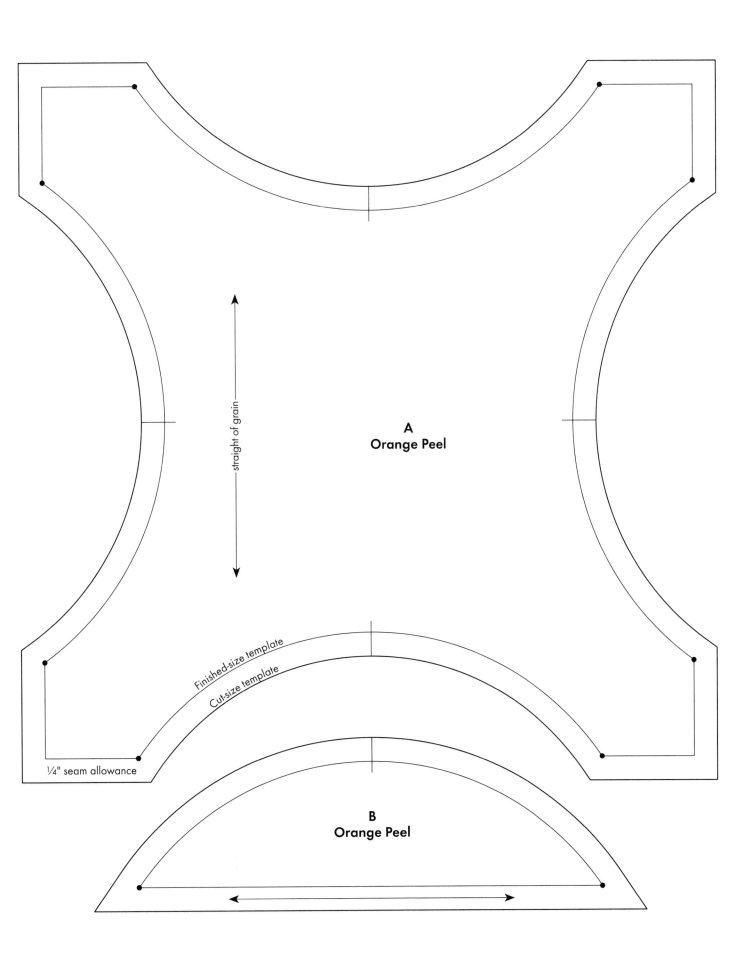

straight of grain

A
Orange Peel

Finished-size template

Cut-size template

¼" seam allowance

B
Orange Peel

Windflowers

Rotating a simple curved unit creates the impression of motion, as if these flowers were blowing in the wind. The secret to success in piecing this simple quilt is that the points of the petals don't touch when you join the blocks. Each block has four petals.

Color photo on page 31.

Project Information at a Glance	
Finished Quilt Size:	32" x 32"
Finished Block Size:	8" x 8"
Finished Border Width:	4"

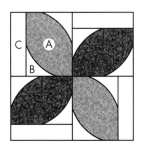

Letters identify templates.

Materials: 44"-wide fabric

1 3/4 yds. cream for background and backing
3/8 yd. medium violet for petals
3/8 yd. dark violet for petals
5/8 yd. lavender for center block and borders
1/3 yd. fuchsia for binding

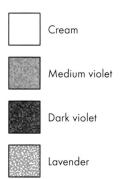

Cream

Medium violet

Dark violet

Lavender

Choosing Fabric

Violets were on my mind when I chose these fabrics. Why don't you try anemones or cosmos colors? Choose petal fabrics with enough contrast to make the flowers read as bi-color.

Recommended Template Style

I used cut-size templates and pieced the entire quilt by machine. See "Template Style" on page 13 and "Curved Piecing by Machine" on page 18.

 The petals are directional. The templates have already been reversed for you. Use them on the wrong side of the fabric, with the printed side of the template up, and your petals will rotate toward the right, as mine do, once they are sewn.

Cutting

All measurements include ¼"-wide seam allowances. Use the templates on page 77.

 Remember to mark the registration marks in the seam allowances and dots where the curved seams start and end.

From the cream fabric, cut:
   3 strips, each 3½" x 42". Crosscut the strip into 32 squares, each 3½" x 3½". Use Template B to mark 2 of Piece B on each square. Cut the curves with scissors to make 64 of Piece B.

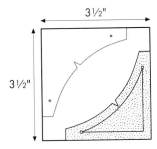

3½"

3½"

   2 strips, each 4½" x 42". Crosscut the strips into 32 rectangles, each 1½" x 4½", for Piece C, or use Template C.

From the medium violet print, cut:
   2 strips, each 4½" x 42". Crosscut the strips into 16 rectangles, each 4½" x 3½". Use Template A to mark the curved lines on the wrong side of each rectangle. Cut the curves with scissors to make 16 of Piece A.

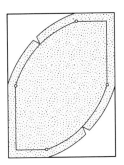

Repeat with the dark violet print to make 16 of Piece A.

From the lavender print, cut:
   1 square, 8½" x 8½", for center block
   2 strips, each 4½" x 24½", for borders
   2 strips, each 4½" x 32½", for borders

From the fuchsia print, cut:
   4 strips, each 2½" x 42", for binding

Block Assembly

1. Sew a Piece B to each side of a Piece A, matching the registration marks and the dots where the curved seams start and end. Make 16 medium violet petals and 16 dark violet petals. Press the seams toward the petals.

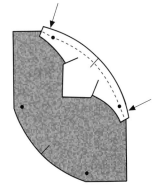

Each unit should measure 3½" x 4½". Block if necessary; see "Blocking Your Blocks" on page 20.

These are elongated curves. Sew across the seam allowances at each end. The seam allowance will press smoothly.

2. Sew a Piece C to the left edge of each curved unit.

3. Assemble each block using 4 petal units, rotating them as shown. Make all the blocks alike, as in the quilt plan, or place the petals randomly, as in the photo on page 31.

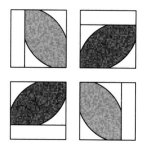
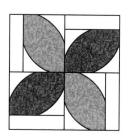

Make 8.

Quilt Assembly

1. Arrange the blocks around the lavender center square as shown in the quilt plan. Join the blocks into rows. Join the rows.
2. Add the 4½" x 24½" border strips to the top and bottom of the quilt top.

3. Add 4½" x 32½" border strips to the sides of the quilt top.

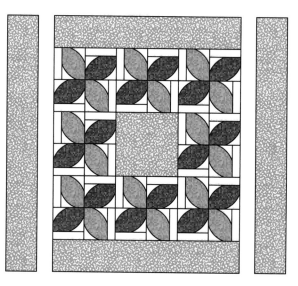

Finishing

1. Layer the quilt top with batting and backing; baste.
2. Quilt by hand or machine. See the quilting suggestion below. *Optional*: Embellish your quilt with buttons at the flower centers.

3. Bind the edges with the fuchsia strips.
4. Add a label to your finished quilt.

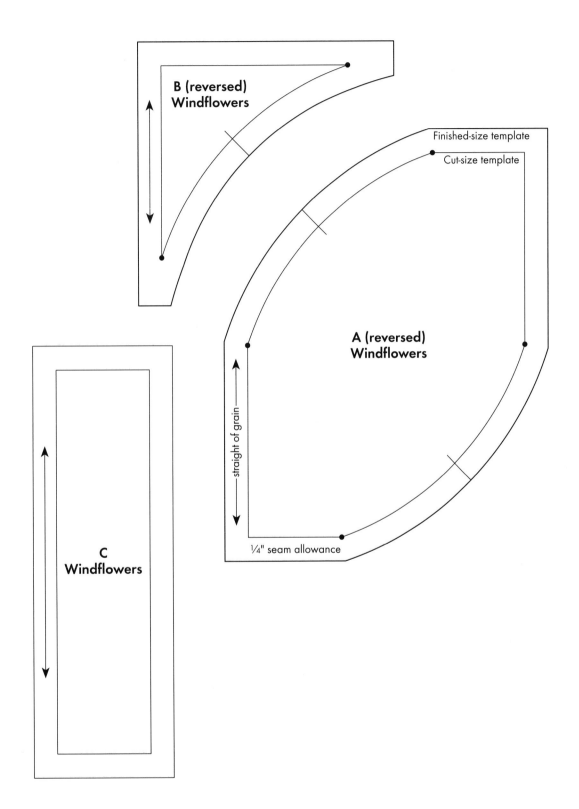

B (reversed)
Windflowers

Finished-size template

Cut-size template

A (reversed)
Windflowers

straight of grain

¼" seam allowance

C
Windflowers

Bibliography

Doak, Carol. *Your First Quilt Book (or it should be!)*. Bothell, Wash.: That Patchwork Place, Inc., 1997.
The best book for beginners.

Flynn, John. *Double Wedding Ring Step-by-Step Workbook*. Billings, Mont.: John Flynn, 1990.
John provides a great quick-piecing system for breaking the wedding ring arc into smaller pieces, as in traditional wedding ring quilts.

Murphy, Anita. *Drunkard's Path: An Easy No-Pins Technique*. San Marcos, Calif.: ASN Publishing, 1991.
Anita instills confidence in piecing a curve by machine and explores the design possibilities of the Drunkard's Path unit.

Schlotzhauer, Joyce. *The Curved Two-Patch System*. McLean, Va.: EPM Publications, Inc., 1982.
A classic curved-piecing system that introduces the concept of designing a gentle, soft curve for easier piecing.

Vlack, Barb. *Too Much Fun*. Bowling Green, Ohio: The Electric Quilt Company, 1997.
Here's an easy way to learn how to design curved patterns on the computer using Electric Quilt.

About the Author

A Nebraska quiltmaker and teacher, Paulette Peters is past president of the Nebraska State Quilt Guild and serves on NSQG's Quilt Preservation Project steering committee. She is a co-founder of Cottonwood Quilters of Nebraska.

She has written three books: *Corners in the Cabin, Borders by Design,* and *Basic Quiltmaking Techniques for Strip Piecing,* all published by That Patchwork Place.

Paulette teaches and lectures across the country, and her work has been included in a number of publications, including *Rotary Riot* and *Make Room for Quilts* (That Patchwork Place), *Quilters Newsletter Magazine,* and *Nebraska Quilts and Quiltmakers* (University of Nebraska Press).

Paulette and her husband, Terry, have a married daughter, two married sons, and a granddaughter who already has her first of many quilts.

Books from Martingale & Company

Appliqué

Appliquilt® Your ABCs
Baltimore Bouquets
Basic Quiltmaking Techniques for Hand Appliqué
Coxcomb Quilt
The Easy Art of Appliqué
Folk Art Animals
From a Quilter's Garden
Stars in the Garden
Sunbonnet Sue All Through the Year
Traditional Blocks Meet Appliqué
Welcome to the North Pole

Borders and Bindings

Borders by Design
The Border Workbook
A Fine Finish
Happy Endings
Interlacing Borders
Traditional Quilts with Painless Borders

Design Reference

All New! Copy Art for Quilters
Blockbender Quilts
Color: The Quilter's Guide
Design Essentials: The Quilter's Guide
Design Your Own Quilts
Freedom in Design
The Log Cabin Design Workbook
The Nature of Design
QuiltSkills
Sensational Settings
Surprising Designs from Traditional Quilt Blocks

Foundation/Paper Piecing

Classic Quilts with Precise Foundation Piecing
Crazy but Pieceable
Easy Machine Paper Piecing
Easy Mix & Match Machine Paper Piecing
Easy Paper-Pieced Keepsake Quilts
Easy Paper-Pieced Miniatures
Easy Reversible Vests
Go Wild with Quilts
Go Wild with Quilts—Again!
A Quilter's Ark
Show Me How to Paper Piece

Hand and Machine Quilting/Stitching

Loving Stitches
Machine Needlelace and Other
    Embellishment Techniques
Machine Quilting Made Easy
Machine Quilting with Decorative Threads
Quilting Design Sourcebook
Quilting Makes the Quilt
Thread Magic
Threadplay with Libby Lehman

Home Decorating

Decorate with Quilts & Collections
The Home Decorator's Stamping Book
Living with Little Quilts
Make Room for Quilts
Soft Furnishings for Your Home
Welcome Home: Debbie Mumm

Miniature/Small Quilts

Beyond Charm Quilts
Celebrate! with Little Quilts
Easy Paper-Pieced Miniatures
Fun with Miniature Log Cabin Blocks
Little Quilts All Through the House
Lively Little Logs
Living with Little Quilts
Miniature Baltimore Album Quilts
No Big Deal
A Silk-Ribbon Album
Small Talk

Needle Arts/Ribbonry

Christmas Ribbonry
Crazy Rags
Hand-Stitched Samplers from I Done My Best
Miniature Baltimore Album Quilts
A Passion for Ribbonry
A Silk-Ribbon Album
Victorian Elegance

Quiltmaking Basics

Basic Quiltmaking Techniques for Hand Appliqué
Basic Quiltmaking Techniques for Strip Piecing
The Joy of Quilting
A Perfect Match
Press for Success
The Ultimate Book of Quilt Labels
Your First Quilt Book (or it should be!)

Rotary Cutting/Speed Piecing

Around the Block with Judy Hopkins
All-Star Sampler
Bargello Quilts
Block by Block
Down the Rotary Road with Judy Hopkins
Easy Star Sampler
Magic Base Blocks for Unlimited Quilt Designs
A New Slant on Bargello Quilts
Quilting Up a Storm
Rotary Riot
Rotary Roundup
ScrapMania
Simply Scrappy Quilts
Square Dance
Stripples
Stripples Strikes Again!
Strips that Sizzle
Two-Color Quilts

Seasonal Quilts

Appliquilt® for Christmas
Christmas Ribbonry
Easy Seasonal Wall Quilts
Folded Fabric Fun
Quilted for Christmas
Quilted for Christmas, Book II
Quilted for Christmas, Book III
Quilted for Christmas, Book IV
Welcome to the North Pole

Surface Design/Fabric Manipulation

15 Beads: A Guide to Creating One-of-a-Kind Beads
The Art of Handmade Paper and Collage
Complex Cloth: A Comprehensive Guide
    to Surface Design
Dyes & Paints: A Hands-On Guide to Coloring Fabric
Hand-Dyed Fabric Made Easy

Theme Quilts

The Cat's Meow
Celebrating the Quilt
Class-Act Quilts
The Heirloom Quilt
Honoring the Seasons
Kids Can Quilt
Life in the Country with Country Threads
Lora & Company
Making Memories
More Quilts for Baby
Once Upon a Quilt
Patchwork Pantry
Quick-Sew Celebrations
Quilted Landscapes
Quilted Legends of the West
Quilts: An American Legacy
Quilts for Baby
Quilts from Nature
Through the Window and Beyond

Watercolor Quilts

Awash with Colour
More Strip-Pieced Watercolor Magic
Strip-Pieced Watercolor Magic
Watercolor Impressions
Watercolor Quilts

Wearables

Crazy Rags
Dress Daze
Dressed by the Best
Easy Reversible Vests
More Jazz from Judy Murrah
Quick-Sew Fleece
Sew a Work of Art Inside and Out
Variations in Chenille

11/98